First World War
and Army of Occupation
War Diary
France, Belgium and Germany

8 DIVISION
23 Infantry Brigade
Duke of Cambridge's Own (Middlesex Regiment)
1/7th Battalion
14 February 1915 - 31 March 1915

WO95/1713/2

The Naval & Military Press Ltd
www.nmarchive.com
Published in association with The National Archives

Published by

The Naval & Military Press Ltd

Unit 10 Ridgewood Industrial Park,

Uckfield, East Sussex,

TN22 5QE England

Tel: +44 (0) 1825 749494

www.naval-military-press.com

www.nmarchive.com

This diary has been reprinted in facsimile from the original. Any imperfections are inevitably reproduced and the quality may fall short of modern type and cartographic standards.

© Crown Copyright
Images reproduced by permission of The National Archives, London, England, 2015.

Contents

Document type	Place/Title	Date From	Date To
Heading	23rd Brigade 8th Division Battalion Transferred To 167th Bde 56th Div 9.2.16 1/7th Battalion Middlesex Regiment January 1916		
Heading	War Diary of 1/7 Middlesex R (T.F) For January 1916 Vol X,XI & XII		
War Diary	Morbecque	01/01/1916	12/01/1916
War Diary	Rue Quesnoy	13/01/1916	18/01/1916
War Diary	La Tranquillite	19/01/1916	26/01/1916
War Diary	Doulieu	27/01/1916	31/01/1916
Heading	23rd Inf. Bde 8th Division War Diary 1/7th Battalion The Middlesex Regiment December 1915		
Heading	War Diary of 1/7th Middlesex Regt. (T.F) From 1st To 31st December 1915 Vol IX		
War Diary	Morbecque	01/12/1915	31/12/1915
Heading	23rd Inf. Bde. 8th Division War Diary 1/7th Battalion The Middlesex Regiment November 1915		
Heading	War Diary of 1/7th Middlesex Regt. (T.F) From 1st November To 30th November 1915 Vol VIII		
War Diary	Fleurbaix	01/11/1915	01/11/1915
War Diary	Bois Grenier	02/11/1915	05/11/1915
War Diary	N.W. of Sailly Bdge	06/11/1915	11/11/1915
War Diary	Bassett House	12/11/1915	23/11/1915
War Diary	Rue Quesnoy	24/11/1915	26/11/1915
War Diary	Morbecque	27/11/1915	30/11/1915
Heading	23rd Inf. Bde. 8th Division War Diary 1/7th Battalion The Middlesex Regiment October 1915		
Heading	War Diary of 1/7th Middlesex R (T.F) For October 1915 Vol VII		
War Diary	La Boutillerie	01/10/1915	05/10/1915
War Diary	La	06/10/1915	10/10/1915
War Diary	Rue De Bruges	11/10/1915	23/10/1915
War Diary	N.W. of Sailly Bridge	24/10/1915	31/10/1915
Heading	23rd Inf. Bde. 8th Division War Diary 1/7th Battalion The Middlesex Regiment September 1915		
Heading	War Diary of 1/7th Middlesex Rgt For September 1915		
War Diary	Rue Du Bois	01/09/1915	05/09/1915
War Diary	Les Haies Basses	06/09/1915	24/09/1915
War Diary	Rouge De Bout	25/09/1915	27/09/1915
War Diary	La Boutillerie	28/09/1915	30/09/1915
Heading	23rd Inf. Bde. 8th Division War Diary 1/7th Battalion The Middlesex Regiment August 1915		
Heading	War Diary of 1/7th Middlesex Regt. For August 1915 Aug-15 Vol VI		
War Diary	Bac St Maur	01/08/1915	07/08/1915
War Diary	Rue Du Moulin	08/08/1915	24/08/1915
War Diary	Rue Du Bois	25/08/1915	31/08/1915
Heading	23rd Inf. Bde. 8th Division War Diary 1/7th Battalion The Middlesex Regiment July 1915		
Heading	8th Division 1/7 Middlesex Vol V From 1st To 31st July 1915		

Type	Description	Start	End
Heading	War Diary of 1/7th Bn Middlesex Regt. From 1st July 1915 To 31st July 1915		
War Diary	La Boutillerie	01/07/1915	06/07/1915
War Diary	Rue De Bruges	07/07/1915	27/07/1915
War Diary	Rue De Quesnes	27/07/1915	31/07/1915
Heading	23 Inf Bde. 8th Division War Diary 1/7th Battalion The Middlesex Regiment June 1915		
Heading	8th Division 1/7th Middlesex Vol IV From 1st To 30th June 1915		
Heading	War Diary of 1/7th Middlesex Regt. From 1st June 1915 To 30th June 1915		
War Diary	Wangerie	01/06/1915	02/06/1915
War Diary	Fauquissart	03/06/1915	08/06/1915
War Diary	Wangerie	09/06/1915	15/06/1915
War Diary	Fauquissart	16/06/1915	22/06/1915
War Diary	Wangerie	23/06/1915	27/06/1915
War Diary	Bac St Maur	28/06/1915	30/06/1915
Heading	23rd Inf. Bde. 8th Division War Diary 1/7th Battalion The Middlesex Regiment May 1915		
Heading	8th Division 1/7th Middlesex Vol III 1-31.5.15		
Heading	War Diary of 1/7th Middlesex Regt. From 1st May 1915 To 31st May 1915		
War Diary	Le Cruseobeau	01/05/1915	02/05/1915
War Diary	La Gorgue	03/05/1915	04/05/1915
War Diary	Rue Du Bois	05/05/1915	10/05/1915
War Diary	La Cordonnerie	10/05/1915	11/05/1915
War Diary	Rue Du Quesnes	12/05/1915	16/05/1915
War Diary	La Cordonnerie	17/05/1915	18/05/1915
War Diary	Wangerie	19/05/1915	21/05/1915
War Diary	Fauquissart	22/05/1915	27/05/1915
War Diary	Wangerie	28/05/1915	31/05/1915
Heading	23rd Inf. Bde. 8th Division War Diary 1/7th Battalion The Middlesex Regiment April 1915		
Heading	8th Division 7th Middlesex Vol II 1-30.4.15		
War Diary	Fleurbaix	01/04/1915	06/04/1915
War Diary	Bac St Maur	07/04/1915	12/04/1915
War Diary	Le Trou	13/04/1915	18/04/1915
War Diary	Rue Du Quesnes	19/04/1915	24/04/1915
War Diary	Le Cruseobeau	25/04/1915	30/04/1915
Heading	23rd Inf. Bde. 8th Divn. Bn. Disembarked Harve from U.K. 13.3.15 War Diary Bn. Joined 3rd Inf. Bde. 15.3.15 1/7th Battalion The Middlesex Regiment 14th February To 31st March 1915		
Heading	1/7th Middlesex Vol I 14.2-31.3.15		
Heading	War Diary of 1/7th Middlesex Regt. From 14th February 1915 To 31st March 1915		
Miscellaneous	1/7th Bn. The Middlesex Regiment		
War Diary	Avonmouth	14/02/1915	14/02/1915
War Diary	High Barret	09/03/1915	12/03/1915
War Diary	Havre	13/03/1915	13/03/1915
War Diary	Le Havre	14/03/1915	14/03/1915
War Diary	La Gorgue	15/03/1915	17/03/1915
War Diary	La Flinque	18/03/1915	21/03/1915
War Diary	La Gorgue	22/03/1915	23/03/1915
War Diary	Bac St Maur	24/03/1915	25/03/1915
War Diary	La Boutillerie	26/03/1915	31/03/1915

Heading   8th Division 23rd Infy Bde 1-7th Bn Middx Regt. Feb 1915-
                Jan 1916 From U.K To 56 Div-167 Bde
Miscellaneous

23rd Brigade.

8th Division.

Battalion transferred to 167th Bde 56th Div 9.2.16.

1/7th BATTALION MIDDLESEX REGIMENT JANUARY 1916.

Army Form C. 2118

8th Div
23rd Bde
5-6

WAR DIARY
or
INTELLIGENCE SUMMARY.
(Erase heading not required.)

CONFIDENTIAL
Duplicate *[signature]*

WAR DIARY
of
1/7 MIDDLESEX R (T.F.)
for January 1916.

Vol X, XI & XII

Place	Date	Hour	Summary of Events and Information	Remarks and references to Appendices

Instructions regarding War Diaries and Intelligence Summaries are contained in F.S. Regs., Part II and the Staff Manual respectively. Title pages will be prepared in manuscript.

Army Form C. 2118.

WAR DIARY
or
INTELLIGENCE SUMMARY.
(Erase heading not required.)

Instructions regarding War Diaries and Intelligence Summaries are contained in F.S. Regs., Part II. and the Staff Manual respectively. Title pages will be prepared in manuscript.

Place	Date	Hour	Summary of Events and Information	Remarks and references to Appendices
MORBECQUE	1.1.16 – 10.1.16		In rest at MORBECQUE. 2/Lt Brown returned from Hospital on 1st Jany. Major S. KING returned from leave on 1st Jany. 2/Lt Moore returned from leave on 3rd Jany. Lt C.P. Chatten & 2/Lt P. Chatten returned from leave on 5th. 2/Lt A.V. Moore reported for duty on the 8th. 2/Lt Kay Brown went on leave on the 10th. In despatches published in London Gazette on Jany 1st the following names were recommended for gallant and distinguished service in the field:- Lt Col E.J. King, Capt & Adjt G.A.W. Bower, Capt S.W. Gillett, Lt A.G. Grazer, Lt G.B. Tait, Lt C. Ashby, No 898 Sgt C.A. Clarke, No 730 Sgt E.J. King, No 1474 Sgt C.P. Reynolds.	[signature]
	11.1.16		The Brigade marched from MORBECQUE via LE PARC, VIERHOEK and VIEUX BERQUIN and billetts in and around ESTAIRES for the night.	
	12.1.16		The Brigade moved into Divisional Reserve in support of trenches line in front of FLEURBAIX the	[signature]

Army Form C. 2118.

WAR DIARY
or
INTELLIGENCE SUMMARY.
(Erase heading not required.)

Instructions regarding War Diaries and Intelligence Summaries are contained in F.S. Regs., Part II. and the Staff Manual respectively. Title pages will be prepared in manuscript.

Place	Date	Hour	Summary of Events and Information	Remarks and references to Appendices
Rue OVESNOY			Battalion moving into Billets on Rue OVESNOY.	
	13.1.16 and 14.1.16		Nothing to record.	
	15.1.16		Conference of C.O.'s at Brigade Office at 10.30 a.m. 2 Lt H.A. WNYMAN reported for duty from England. Brigade Machine Gun Company was formed this day. Lt Tait & 23 N.C.O's and men being transferred to it. Coy Commanders & Batt- Staff visited trenches to be taken over on 16th. 2 Lt Sherlock went on leave.	
"	16.1.16		Nothing to record	
"	17.1.16		2 Lt Woodrofe went on leave. Conference of C.O's at Bne Office at 10.30 a.m. 2 Lt J.D.M. Smith returned from Machine Gun School at St OMER and assumed command of Machine Gun Section which was renamed with Lewis Guns on the 12th in place of 4 maxims turned in to Ordnance. In the London Gazette of Capt J.C.M. Smith was promoted Major, & Lt R.Wilkinson Capt, & 2 Lt R.M.E. King & all dated 2nd Nov.	

Army Form C. 2118.

WAR DIARY
or
INTELLIGENCE SUMMARY.
(Erase heading not required.)

Place	Date	Hour	Summary of Events and Information	Remarks and references to Appendices
RŒUFNOY	18.1.16		The Battn relieved the 2 LINCOLNS in sections N41 & N51 of the Trenches — B Coy and two Lewis guns in N41. D two platoons in N51. One platoon of D Coy in MILL ROAD Post. Battn H.Q. in the DAVID. An advanced platoon of A Coy at BASSE'T HOUSE. The Remainder of the Battn relieved the 1st London Regt in the Reserve. H.Q. at FLEURBAIX. Two companies the 2 platoons in sections Relieved at CROIX de ROME with 2 Lewis guns. One platoon & 1 Lewis gun occupied CAIN trenches formerly ABEL post. he Trenches hit. The 2 West Yorks were on our left. On our right a Battn of the 70 Bde. A section of Bde Machine gun coy was in N41. & another gun in MILL ROAD Post.	
LA TRANOUILLITE	19.1.16		Early in morning a patrol under Lce Cpl STOTT (D coy) came into contact with another German patrol and drove it in. Lce Cpl STOTT being wounded.	
	20.1.16		Pte DEAMER (B coy) accidentally wounded.	
	21.1.16		Major Smith & 2Lt G.R. King went on leave.	

WAR DIARY or INTELLIGENCE SUMMARY

Army Form C. 2118.

Place	Date	Hour	Summary of Events and Information	Remarks and references to Appendices
LA TRAMQUILITE	22.1.16		Two companies + two guns in Bde Reserve relieved the companies holding the trenches, C Coy taking over N41 & G3 N51 and M42 Redoubt whilst D Coy finished and drew Platoons at BASSÉE tournant. The 2 Scottish Rifles were on our right & the 7th Bde on our left.	
do	23.1.16		2 Lt P. Challen went to the Bde Grenadier School. At 5am a patrol of 5 men from C Coy under Serjt E.D.F. moved out to the German lines + lay down about 50 yards from their line. After 20 minutes 3 Germans came over the parapet towards them. They waited until they were about 15 yards from them + threw a bomb into the midst of them which failed to explode. They then opened fire + shot down one of the enemy, but observing a fresh hostile patrol of some approaching on their right flank they fell back rapidly + returned in safety.	
do	24.1.16	Between 2 + 2.30 pm	the neighbourhood of M49 was heavily shelled there was one direct hit on the buildings.	

WAR DIARY
or
INTELLIGENCE SUMMARY.

(Erase heading not required.)

Army Form C. 2118.

Place	Date	Hour	Summary of Events and Information	Remarks and references to Appendices
LA TRANQUILLITE	24.1.16 cont.		At 7.15 p.m. a/c. F.D/Smith was mortally wounded in the trenches. He had just laid his machine gun on a spot from where the enemy had been sending up lights runs about to open fire when he was shot through the head. About a patrol of 4 men under Cpl. Edge moving up towards the German lines heard two strong German patrols moving towards them down each side of the ditch along which they were advancing. The night was pitch dark & very foggy so that nothing could be seen but presumably the two patrols were of the same strength as has been usual lately in the case of German patrols namely from 8 to 10 men each. Cpl. Edge waited for the enemy to come up to him, he then threw two bombs into the patrol on the further side of the stream which at once fled: he next turned on the other patrol which at once fell back, they followed after	

Army Form C. 2118.

WAR DIARY
or
INTELLIGENCE SUMMARY.
(Erase heading not required.)

Instructions regarding War Diaries and Intelligence Summaries are contained in F. S. Regs., Part II. and the Staff Manual respectively. Title pages will be prepared in manuscript.

Place	Date	Hour	Summary of Events and Information	Remarks and references to Appendices
LA TRANQUILITÉ 24.11.1915 (contd)			after, but were unable to catch it up before the Germans reached their barbed wire	
do.	25.1.16		An artillery demonstration was made against the enemy lines on our right front from 12.30 p.m. to 3 p.m. The enemy retaliated & the neighbourhood of H.Q. was heavily shelled from 2.30 p.m. to 4.30 p.m. A message was received from the field Ambulance to say that 2/Lt. F.R. Smith died at 1.35 A.M. 2/Lt. Troutloffe returned from leave. 2/Lt. E.A. Brown took over his duties as Commandant of Brigade Trench Mortar School.	
do.	26.1.16		The Battalion was relieved in the Trenches by the 2nd. West Yorkshire Regt. Moved back to Bulien in relief to enable the 1st Tyneside Scottish to take their place in the trenches for Instructional purposes. Whilst at Bulien, at 11.30 A.M. Major E.J. FROST, who had visited "C" lines for the purpose of placing crosses over the graves of	

WAR DIARY
or
INTELLIGENCE SUMMARY.
(Erase heading not required.)

Army Form C. 2118.

Place	Date	Hour	Summary of Events and Information	Remarks and references to Appendices
LA TRANQUILLITÉ	26.1.16 (cont)		the men buried there was shot through the head by a German sniper: the Irish Guards in whose lines he was sent him to the 9th Field Ambulance at ESTAIRES where he died shortly after arrival. 2/Lt. Sherlock returned from leave. Capt. Gregory proceeded to England where his place being taken by Capt Ordish R.A.M.C. 26th Field Ambulance.	
DOULIEU	27.1.16		Day of rest: Major Hudson & Lt. Beatson proceeded on leave.	
do	28.1.16		Three working parties each of two officers & 80 men for work under R.E. under communication avenues. They were despatched at 5.30 p.m. to CROIX MARÉCHAL, CROIX BLANCHE & WINDY POST respectively.	
do	29.1.16		Working parties the same as yesterday same time & places. 2/Lt. P. Challen returned from Bomb School & took command of the Machine Gun Section. 2/Lt. G.A. King returned from leave.	

Army Form C. 2118.

WAR DIARY
or
INTELLIGENCE SUMMARY.
(Erase heading not required.)

Instructions regarding War Diaries and Intelligence Summaries are contained in F. S. Regs., Part II. and the Staff Manual respectively. Title pages will be prepared in manuscript.

Place	Date	Hour	Summary of Events and Information	Remarks and references to Appendices
DOULIEU	30.1.16		Working parties as usual.	
"	31.1.16		2Lt G.A. King dispatched to Trench Mortar School. Working parties as before except parties reduced from 88 to 70.	

Sgd. ......
Lt Col
Cmdg 1/7 Middx R (T.F.)

Sgd. Howe
Cpt M/J
1/7 Middx R (T.F.)

23rd Inf. Bde.
8th Division

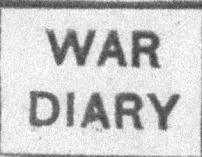

1/7th Battalion,

THE MIDDLESEX REGIMENT,

DECEMBER 1915.

Army Form C. 2118.

8th

WAR DIARY
or
INTELLIGENCE SUMMARY.
(Erase heading not required.)

CONFIDENTIAL

WAR DIARY.

of 1/7th Middlesex Regt (T.F.)

from 1st to 31st December 1915.

Vol IX

Army Form C. 2118.

WAR DIARY
or
INTELLIGENCE SUMMARY.
(Erase heading not required.)

Instructions regarding War Diaries and Intelligence Summaries are contained in F. S. Regs., Part II. and the Staff Manual respectively. Title pages will be prepared in manuscript.

Place	Date	Hour	Summary of Events and Information	Remarks and references to Appendices
MORECAMBE	1.xii.15 to 11.xii.15		Time devoted to Platoon, Company & Battn training. Lt Shipton went on leave on 8th Dec.	
	12.xii.15			
do.	13.xii.15 - 19.xii.15		Battn engaged in training. Lt Wilkinson went on leave.	

Gort(?)

Army Form C. 2118.

WAR DIARY
or
INTELLIGENCE SUMMARY.
(Erase heading not required.)

Instructions regarding War Diaries and Intelligence Summaries are contained in F. S. Regs., Part II. and the Staff Manual respectively. Title pages will be prepared in manuscript.

Place	Date	Hour	Summary of Events and Information	Remarks and references to Appendices
	20.XII.15		17th Dec. Lt Shipton returned from leave on 14th Dec. Lt Brown went into hospital on 18th inst. The Battalion started on Divisional Manoeuvres marching through SERCUS, LYNDE and WARDRECQUES & RACQUINGHEM. Distance 11 miles. Started 9.45 a.m. arrived at destination at 4 p.m.	off map 5A HAZEBROUCK 1/100,000
	21.XII.15		Marched at Head of main body through CAUCHIE D'ECOUES, THEROUANNE, DELETTE to level crossing - inch through DELETTE, through ERNY ST. JULIEN when it deployed to attack on Hill 161 in cooperation with main attack of 23 Inf. Bde on BOMY. The 25th Brigade on its left attacking CUHEM. Returned to Billets at ERNY ST JULIEN that theoretically held for the right. No II section of Battle outpost line from BERGUIGNY (incl) to CUHEM-BEATMETZ road (excl). Distance marched 14½ miles. Raining all day. Started 7.45 a.m. got into Billets 5.0 p.m.	
	22.X.ii.15		Marched back through THEROUANNE - CAUCHIE D'ECOUES	

Army Form C. 2118.

WAR DIARY
or
INTELLIGENCE SUMMARY.
(Erase heading not required.)

Instructions regarding War Diaries and Intelligence Summaries are contained in F. S. Regs., Part II. and the Staff Manual respectively. Title pages will be prepared in manuscript.

Place	Date	Hour	Summary of Events and Information	Remarks and references to Appendices
MORBECQUE.			No Billets at WARDRECQUES. Billeting area was found to be occupied by LAHORE Division. Leave sent forward to find Billets at CAMPAGNE. Distance covered 12½ miles. Started at 10.30 a.m. arrived in Billets at 4.30 p.m. Raining most of the day.	
	23.XII.15		marched back to Camp at MORBECQUE through WARDRECQUES - BLARINGHEM - LE CROQUET + LA BELLE HOTESSE. Distance 11 miles. Started at 8.0 a.m. arrived in Camp 12.30 p.m.	
	23.12.15 - 31.12.15		Rest Camp at Morbecque. Major S. King went on leave Dec 24th. 2/Lt. Mode on 28th. 2/Lt. P. Chillen + Lt. O.F. Challen on 31st. Lt. A.R. Williamson returned from leave on 31st. Major Frost returned to duty from England on Dec. 25th.	

B.W.J. Lt Col
 Comdg 1/7 Middx R
 (T.F.)

Javier Power
Captain Mr
1/7 Middx R
(T.F.)

23rd Inf. Bde.
8th Division.

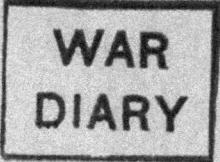

1/7th Battalion

THE MIDDLESEX REGIMENT

NOVEMBER 1915.

Army Form C. 2118.

WAR DIARY
or
INTELLIGENCE SUMMARY.
(Erase heading not required.)

CONFIDENTIAL

WAR DIARY.

of 1/7th Middlesex Regt (T.F.)

from 1st November to 30th November
1915.

Vol VIII

Army Form C. 2118.

WAR DIARY
or
INTELLIGENCE SUMMARY.
(Erase heading not required.)

Instructions regarding War Diaries and Intelligence Summaries are contained in F.S. Regs., Part II. and the Staff Manual, respectively. Title pages will be prepared in manuscript.

Place	Date	Hour	Summary of Events and Information	Remarks and references to Appendices
FLEURBAIX	1/Nov/1915		Took over trenches North of BOIS GRENIER from 2 Devons. The trenches were held by D, A & C Coys, in order from right to left, and the machine gun section, H.Q. and 2/B Coy were at WHITE CITY, remainder of B Coy being distributed, one platoon in STANNAWAY POST, 2 sections in EMMA POST and 2 sections in the old cork hut.	
BOIS GRENIER	2 Nov. 1915		General Hudson and General Trew inspected the trenches. Our sharpshooters shot two Germans.	
	3 Nov. 1915.		Our sharpshooters shot two Germans. One man wounded.	
	4 Nov/9/15.		Early in the morning a patrol of 3 Germans was seen outside their wire, we shot down two, the other got away, one being wounded. General Twegu went round the trenches in the morning. In the evening the Battn was relieved by the 1st Sherwood Foresters and went into Brigade Reserve, Rn.R. LYS, N.W. of SAILLY BRIDGE, being in Divisional Reserve. ATHOS two found with W. Yorks Transport.	

1577 Wt.W10791/1773 500,000 1/15 D.D.&L.   A.D.S.S./Forms/C. 2118.

Army Form C. 2118.

WAR DIARY
or
INTELLIGENCE SUMMARY.
(Erase heading not required.)

Instructions regarding War Diaries and Intelligence Summaries are contained in F.S. Regs., Part II. and the Staff Manual respectively. Title pages will be prepared in manuscript.

Place	Date	Hour	Summary of Events and Information	Remarks and references to Appendices
N.W of SAILLY Bdge	6.XI.15		A day nothing party of 100 men was furnished. Nothing to record.	
	7.XI.15		Capt Gillett returned from leave.	
	8.XI.15		Batt⁰ furnished working parties amounting to 425 men.	
	9.XI.15		Scheme of events of offensive operations submitted to Brigade. Orders received for Right Brigade area on night of 9/11th. Orders received for Major L.R. King to proceed to England to take command of 9th Service Battalion and for Capt T.M. Cozzer to report to ROUEN, Central Requisition office for 2 months probation.	
	10.XI.15		C.O. & Adjut Capt Maitland (pros. Edn. over our Accountancy. fork over Command of 9 Coy) went on leave. Capt T.M. Cozzer left for ROUEN. Capt Smith acts Adjutant, waited BASSETT HOUSE (N4 a 2.3) to arrange for the 1/8 Midd⁰ relief. Sept 16 the 70th over command of no army. Major L.R. King left for England. Batt⁰ relieves Middlk sheet 36. Bn in trenches C Coy being in N41 and A Coy in N 57 with a 3rd Sqn platoon in MILL Road hole. B Coy more in Crx BLANCHE post scale 1/40,000. and D Coy in Billets at CROIX BLANCHE. Two machine guns were	BELGIUM and FRANCE Bsorino

| | 11.XI.15 | | | |

1577 Wt.W10791/1773 500,000 1/15 D.D.&L. A.D.S.S./Forms/C. 2118.

Army Form C. 2118.

WAR DIARY
or
INTELLIGENCE SUMMARY.
(Erase heading not required.)

Instructions regarding War Diaries and Intelligence Summaries are contained in F. S. Regs., Part II. and the Staff Manual respectively. Title pages will be prepared in manuscript.

Place	Date	Hour	Summary of Events and Information	Remarks and references to Appendices
BASSETT HOUSE	12.XI.15		In the trenches – 2 in CROIX BLANCHE Post. 2 Scottish Rifles were on the right and 2 Devons on the left. Drafts of 25 Other Ranks arrived from neighbourhood of ARRAS where they had been attached to digging Battalion.	
	13.XI.15		Nothing to Report.	
	14.XI.15		Brigade Commander visited the trenches. Alarmed by rifle fire the war Dog ATHOS disappeared. Hospital found.	
	15.XI.15		Major S. King returned from leave. Sharp notices that on Germans B Coy relieved C Coy & D Coy A Coy. C Coy bivouacked CROIX BLANCHE Post & A Coy were supporting Coy in Billets at CROIX BLANCHE.	
	16.XI.15		The Brigade Commander accompanied by C.O.E visited trenches. The neighbourhood that of Germans.	
	17.XI.15		The Snipers notes the Germans.	
	18.XI.15		General Haldane visited the trenches.	
	19.XI.15		C.O. returned from leave.	

Army Form C. 2118.

WAR DIARY or INTELLIGENCE SUMMARY.

(Erase heading not required.)

Place	Date	Hour	Summary of Events and Information	Remarks and references to Appendices
BASSETT HOUSE	20.XI.1915		An artillery demonstration supported by machine guns was made on German trenches in neighbourhood of some DERANGES. Artillery Bombardments took place from 11.30 – 11.45 am, 1.30 – 1.45 pm and for 5 minutes at 7 pm & 8.15 pm. Our two machine guns in trenches operated to think machine gun was brought up from CROIX BLANCHE to position in rear of convent hall from which indirect fire was brought to bear on some de la MARLIQUE. The Germans retaliated on our trenches and on MILL Road Post St Yves, and were being wounded. Capt Tully returned from England today, and to other commands of C Company; Shropshire killed one German. 8th leave to officers stopped for the present.	
	21.XI.1915		General Turon visited trenches HQ. Shropshires killed one German.	
	22.XI.1915		The trenches hire today are ready in led the frontiers to to right	

Army Form C. 2118.

WAR DIARY
or
INTELLIGENCE SUMMARY.
(Erase heading not required.)

Instructions regarding War Diaries and Intelligence Summaries are contained in F. S. Regs., Part II. and the Staff Manual respectively. Title pages will be prepared in manuscript.

Place	Date	Hour	Summary of Events and Information	Remarks and references to Appendices
BASSETT House			9ᵗʰ DEVON avenue was handed over to the Scottish Rifles. The platoon of "C" Coy so relieved relieved A Coy in MILL Road post. B Coy took over from the 2 Devons the portion of trenches line between CONVENT avenue and the Bᵈ of TINTERIE Road holding it with 3 platoons dividing the front platoons equally between FORAY post and BOTTLERY post. "A" Coy prolonged its left to CONVENT avenue with its platoons from MILL Road post. Another gun was moved up from CROIX BLANCHE to a position in the trenches near the junction of N52 and N53	
	23.XI.15		The Battⁿ was relieved by the 6ᵗʰ Ox & Bucks L.I. and went into billets in the rue QUESNOY. During the morning Lt. General Pulteney commanding III Corps accompanied by Mjr Genl Romer visited the trenches.	
Rue QUESNOY	24.XI.15	At 2.30 p.m.	the Battⁿ marched via SAILLY and ESTAIRES to NEUF BERQUIN and went into billets near VIEUX MOULIN and became part of Corps Reserve.	

Army Form C. 2118.

WAR DIARY
or
INTELLIGENCE SUMMARY.
(Erase heading not required.)

Instructions regarding War Diaries and Intelligence Summaries are contained in F.S. Regs., Part II. and the Staff Manual respectively. Title pages will be prepared in manuscript.

Place	Date	Hour	Summary of Events and Information	Remarks and references to Appendices
	25.XI.15		The Battalion remained resting at NEUF BERQUIN. A party of 12 N.C.O's then per company under Lt Shipton was despatched to MORBECQUE at 9.15 am to take over huts+tents.	
	26.XI.15		The Battalion marched off at 7.30 am and moving via LA COURONNE, LA MOTTE and LE TIR ANGLAIS went into Camp N of MORBECQUE. The Inspection ordered by the Commander in chief for 2 p.m. was cancelled owing to the weather.	
MORBECQUE	27.XI.15		Stores previously dumped at SAILLY fetched from STEEN BECQUE. Day spent in getting Camp straight, its Huts, Bivouacs and Ronder thing returned from leave.	
do	28.XI.15		Conference of C.O.'s at 10 a.m.	
	29.XI.15		Time devoted to Platoon, Company + Battn Training	
	30.XI.15		2Lt J. D. M. Smith rejoined on 30.15.	

BJ VBJ Wood
Aug 1/7 Middx R (T.F.)

Sir F Lowes
Capt M.
1/7 Middx R (T.F.)

23rd Inf. Bde
8th Division

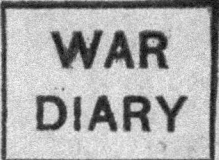

1/7th Battalion,

THE MIDDLESEX REGIMENT

OCTOBER 1915.

Army Form C. 2118.

WAR DIARY
or
INTELLIGENCE SUMMARY.
(Erase heading not required.)

CONFIDENTIAL.

War Diary
of
1/7th Middlesex R. (T.F.)
for October 1915.

Vol VII

Army Form C. 2118

WAR DIARY
or
INTELLIGENCE SUMMARY
(Erase heading not required.)

Instructions regarding War Diaries and Intelligence Summaries are contained in F. S. Regs., Part II. and the Staff Manual respectively. Title Pages will be prepared in manuscript.

Place	Date	Hour	Summary of Events and Information	Remarks and references to Appendices
LA BOUTILLERIE	1-10-15		General TUSON again visited trenches. "A" & "C" Coys were relieved by "D" & "B" Coy respectively. "C" Coy going to CROIX BLANCHE and "A" Coy into Brigade Reserve at CROIX BLANCHE. Machine Gun section was relieved by 2 guns on Bn. Reserve. No. 24002 Sergt. M. A. NORTHORPE + No 1897 Pte. J. FLOWER were killed this day. Sharpshooters killed 3 Germans.	
	2-10-15		Down an enemy dead.	
	3-10-15		C.O. attended B.de Conference at 11 am. Sharpshooters	
	4-10-15		2 L.H. Channels returned totally with the Battn. from the Bombing Grenadier School two replaced by 2 Lieut Brown. But sharpshooters shot one German and wounded one prisoner.	
	5.10.15		General Hudson accompanied by Genl. Tuson inspected the trenches this morning. In the evening "D" & "A" companies were relieved by "A" and "C" companies respectively. "D" Coy occupied CROIX BLANCHE fort and "C" company as supporting company at CROIX BLANCHE. "B" Coy went into trenches. As trenches were changed, Sharpshooters shot one German machine gun team. Two periscopes and one rifle to periscope.	Casualties Copy 1894

Army Form C. 2118

WAR DIARY
or
INTELLIGENCE SUMMARY

(Erase heading not required.)

Instructions regarding War Diaries and Intelligence Summaries are contained in F.S. Regs., Part II. and the Staff Manual respectively. Title Pages will be prepared in manuscript.

Place	Date	Hour	Summary of Events and Information	Remarks and references to Appendices
LA	6.10.15		News received of a fresh French advance in CHAMPAGNE. It Tait went on leave. Sharpshooters	
	7.10.15		General Munro visited the trenches. Sharpshooters accounted for 6 Germans and one periscope. Capt Smith went on leave.	
	8.10.15		Trenches reconnoitred at 10.30 am and re-taken over at 3.30 pm. There were no casualties. Sharpshooters accounted for 3 Germans and 2 periscopes.	
	9.10.15		During the night a patrol under Lieut Edge went out to the German lines and owing to the darkness fell into a hostile saphead at the moment unoccupied. They brought back a cushion as a trophy. Shortly after the patrol Lnd/Cpl Lough had two bombs thrown into it by the enemy. During the afternoon Brigadier General Tuson again visited the trenches. Sharpshooters shot 4 Germans.	
	10.10.15		The Battalion was relieved in the trenches, the right company by the 3/Manch, and the left company by the 2 East Lancs. Cross of BLANCHE post was relieved by 5/Manchesters the supporting company by a company of the Worcesters. The Battalion went into billets on the Rue Jean... Cap...	

WAR DIARY
or
INTELLIGENCE SUMMARY.

(Erase heading not required.)

Army Form C. 2118.

Place	Date	Hour	Summary of Events and Information	Remarks and references to Appendices
Rue du BRUGET	10.10.15		During the 13 days in the trenches we had 3 men killed & 2 wounded whilst its Sharpshooters inflicted 21 casualties on the enemy in addition to any caused by chance shots. During the previous tour of duty in the trenches we had 9 killed & 7 wounded whilst our Sharpshooters inflicted 40 casualties on the enemy. Account of the Sharpshooters two nets follows:— Penalty.	
			Germans	
			L/Sgt Reynolds 3 3	
			Cpl Philcott 11 1	
			Cpl Reynolds 5 —	
			Cpl Clark 1 2	
			Pte Church 1 3	
			Lt. C. F. Challen — 1	
			21 10	
Rue du BRUGET	11.10.15		A day of rest. Night working party of 20 ordered to furnish to work under E&L.O 1st FARM and 1st Kent Counties R.E.	
	12.10.15		Nothing to report.	

WAR DIARY
INTELLIGENCE SUMMARY

Army Form C. 2118.

Place	Date	Hour	Summary of Events and Information	Remarks and references to Appendices
	13-10-15		About 3 p.m. 2/Lt. Scott who was in the trenches near Chapigny in command of a Trench Mortar Battery was mortally wounded. He was at the time attached to the 61st Inf. Bde. and was taken back to their Field Ambulance at Estaires where he died about 7 p.m. without recovering consciousness. The Battery had been taking part in a demonstration in co-operation with offensive movements further south. It was just packing up ready to move out of the trenches when a high explosive shell fell in the midst of the personnel of the Battery, killing or wounding the whole. Major L. Col. Illing and Capt. Bowen went on leave. L. Tait returned from leave.	
	14-10-15		Capt. Smith returned from leave. Lt. Scott was buried today on the RUE PETILLON between Laventie. Stacey's funeral. At 10 a.m. the C.O. & Adjutant attended a conference at Brigade Headquarters with reference to taking over huts from the 24th Brigade. A working party of 150 men was furnished for work on the Corps area Tramway and 150 men for work in the neighbourhood of ELBOW FARM.	
	15-10-15			
	16-10-15		Company Commanders & Machine Gun Officer went to look over trenches before taking over. One Officer (2/Lt Grover) went to lay a communiqué for the Legion of Honour and one N.C.O (Sgt C.A. Clarke) for the Legion de Guerre.	[signature]

Army Form C. 2118.

WAR DIARY
or
INTELLIGENCE SUMMARY.
(Erase heading not required.)

Instructions regarding War Diaries and Intelligence Summaries are contained in F.S. Regs., Part II. and the Staff Manual respectively. Title pages will be prepared in manuscript.

Place	Date	Hour	Summary of Events and Information	Remarks and references to Appendices
	17-10-15		Battalion took over trenches N.4.1 and N.5.1. also Mill Posts from 5th Black Watch. "D" Coy. taking over right of the line and "B" Coy Clear and flected) the left. the morning Platoon of "D" Coy manning Mill Res. Post. Two machine guns placed in def trenches. Batn. Hd Qrs at Braan House. The remainder of the Batn. was billeted at CROIX BLANCHE. "A" Coy. acting as garrison and furnishing the Post and "C" Coy not normally machine gun being in support of trench garrison. Surgeon Capt. Andrews, Commdr R.S.F. joined, in place of Capt. Gregory, R.A.M.C. Gone on leave.	
	18-10-15		Sharp rifle fire was in answer to S.O.S. call from the Belton. on our right. At 9.55 pm this was on turned out to be unnecessary. Capt. Gregory, R.A.M.C. went on leave. The Brigadier inspected the trenches in the morning.	
	19-10-15			
	20-10-15		The Brigadier inspected & approved the position selected for advanced Battalion Head Quarters. Capt. Woodly & Lieut. Gosset rejoined the Battalion. Our sharp shooters inflicted three casualties on the Enemy.	

Army Form C.2118.

WAR DIARY
or
INTELLIGENCE SUMMARY.
(Erase heading not required.)

Instructions regarding War Diaries and Intelligence Summaries are contained in F. S. Regs., Part II. and the Staff Manual respectively. Title pages will be prepared in manuscript.

Place	Date	Hour	Summary of Events and Information	Remarks and references to Appendices
	21.10.15		Our Sharpshooters accounted for three of the enemy	
	22.10.15		Our Sharpshooters accounted for one of the enemy.	
	23.10.15		Our Sharpshooters accounted for two of the enemy. During the afternoon the left company was shelled with shrapnel. No casualty by S.M. Fire. In the evening the Battn was relieved by the 16th Middlesex and went into billets N.W. of SAILLY BRIDGE.	
N.W. of SAILLY BAR	24.10.15		Major L.R. King and Capt Bower returned from leave. Conference of Commanding Officers at 11 a.m. During the 6 days we were in the trenches we had 4 men wounded, none severely, whereas our Sharpshooters inflicted 10 casualties on the enemy for certain.	
do	25.10.15		Church Parade 11.30 a.m. Another Conference of Commanding Officers in the afternoon.	
do	26.10.15		Orders received to move to FLEURBAIX tomorrow.	

Capt & Adjt

1577 Wt.W10791/1773 500,000 1/15 D.D.&L. A.D.S.S./Forms/C. 2118.

Army Form C. 2118.

WAR DIARY
or
INTELLIGENCE SUMMARY.
(Erase heading not required.)

Instructions regarding War Diaries and Intelligence Summaries are contained in F. S. Regs., Part II. and the Staff Manual respectively. Title pages will be prepared in manuscript.

Hour, Date, Place	Summary of Events and Information	Remarks and references to Appendices
27.10.15	The battn. moved into billets round FLEURBAIX forming the left battn. of the Brigade Reserve, the Brigade holding the trenches S. of BOIS GRENIER. HQ. at FLEURBAIX, B Coy at PORT a CLOUS farm C Coy machine gun section (less 2 guns) at LA TOULETTE, D Coy in the DELETTREE with a guard in chisel pits. A Coy formed supporting Coy of 2ndt Bn. Irish rifles trench holders in Rue du CHARLES with one platoon keeping the Grenadier Section holding BOIS GRENIER Post. Remaining two machine guns were at WHITE City and EMMA Post respectively then day ATHOS disappeared toss. Coy offpys returned from leave. Scott	
28.10.15	Quiet day. Working party of 1 NCO + 10 men not found. A night working party of 200 found. Scott	Scott Jones Capt Adjt

(73989) W.14141-463. 400,000. 9/14. H. & J., Ltd. Forms/C. 2118/10.

Army Form C. 2118.

WAR DIARY
or
INTELLIGENCE SUMMARY.
(Erase heading not required.)

Instructions regarding War Diaries and Intelligence Summaries are contained in F. S. Regs., Part II. and the Staff Manual respectively. Title pages will be prepared in manuscript.

Place	Date	Hour	Summary of Events and Information	Remarks and references to Appendices
	29.10.15		Explained to Company Commanders (10.30am) measures to be taken in case of attack and indicated all officers reconnoitre towards routes leading to trenches S. of BOIS GRENIER. C.O. attended conference at Bde H.Q. 4.30pm, hoping of 2nd new front.	
	30.10.15		C.O. attended conference at de Hâa before going into Divisional Reserve on 21 Nov. maj S. King, S/S Hospital. Orders received	
	31.10.15		C.O. and Adjutant reconnoitred posts trenches S. of BOIS GRENIER, attended day orders received cancelling yesterdays. At 6.30pm meeting of Coys 2Dsons in trenches instead. Coys to move tomorrow morning nothing of any Coys to explain tomorrows relief.	

B. V. Johan
Maj. 1/7 Middlesex R
(T.F.)

[signature]
Capt & Adjt.
1/7 Middlesex
(T.F.)

23rd Inf. Bde.
8th Division

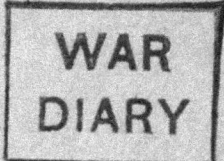

1/7th Battalion

THE MIDDLESEX REGIMENT

SEPTEMBER 1915

Army Form C. 2118.

WAR DIARY
or
INTELLIGENCE SUMMARY.
(Erase heading not required.)

CONFIDENTIAL

War Diary
of 1/7 Middlesex Regt
for September 1915

Army Form C. 2118

WAR DIARY
or
INTELLIGENCE SUMMARY
(Erase heading not required.)

Instructions regarding War Diaries and Intelligence Summaries are contained in F.S. Regs., Part II. and the Staff Manual respectively. Title Pages will be prepared in manuscript.

Place	Date	Hour	Summary of Events and Information	Remarks and references to Appendices
Puiton Bois	1.9.15		During the evening C & D coys relieved A & B coys in trenches afterwards of D Coy taking over MILL ROAD POST. A & B coys went into Billets at CROIX BLANCHE B Coy providing the extra E. post.	
	2.9.15		Our snipers could not fire anything. 2th Worcesters relieved us to-morrow. Our snipers could not find anything to shoot at. 1st Shipton + 2nd Scott returned from leave. The sharpshooters shewed one periscope.	
"	3.9.15			
"	4.9.15		All quiet in trenches nothing to report. The sharpshooters shot one German.	
"	5.9.15		Battn was relieved by the 7th King's O. Yorks L.I. moved into Bivouac Rearve at LES HAIES BASSES.	
LES HAIES BASSES	6.9.15		Rest day. The General Clarke left to take up an appointment with the 12th Corps. Lt Col J.G. Co. Sylvance took Officers detail. Samplaine. Maj. S. King returned to duty from hospital.	
"	7.9.15		Brigadier General TYSON, N.A. assumed command of the Brigade from this date.	

Army Form C. 2118

WAR DIARY
or
INTELLIGENCE SUMMARY
(Erase heading not required.)

Instructions regarding War Diaries and Intelligence Summaries are contained in F. S. Regs., Part II. and the Staff Manual respectively. Title Pages will be prepared in manuscript.

Place	Date	Hour	Summary of Events and Information	Remarks and references to Appendices
LES HAIES BASSES	8.9.15		A draft of 75 Men trans arrived. Two Companies kept safe tranching this entrenchment. this position to trenching forward appealing to, close materials reported and respect with. The following two received from the Bde. 2nd Bin No. 59(A). Near Luentin 23 1 Bg Ane. Late reference hypn: No C/B/4 dated 3rd Septr 1915. MY.O.C. wishes to stake on... given by... Privates Prentice and Drennan Ferguson... He also wishes his appreciation of their cordial courage to the Patrol and Stretcher bearers as about. (Sgd) R.G. Scarlett Cpt. W. Leal. P.H. R.H.G. E. 3/7/15 O.C. Thistle... R... Kent I Torrance...	

1875 Wt. W593/826 1,000,000 4/15 J.B.C. & A. A.D.S.S./Forms/C.2118.

Army Form C. 2118

WAR DIARY
or
INTELLIGENCE SUMMARY
(Erase heading not required.)

Place	Date	Hour	Summary of Events and Information	Remarks and references to Appendices
LES HAMES BASSES	8.9.15		Application of the G.O.C. in Course of Application Hope of May Philosophers Women's Lyceum. The conduct of Rifles and Kitchen Review was on this order to observe.	
			(sgd) Travers Clarke Brig Genl And 23rd Infantry Bgde	
	9.9.15		4/IX/15. Major & Reply attended conference of the GOC today. Paraded as for GO today. 2nd & 3rd May thrown half a leave.	
	10.9.15		Companies paraded as for yesterday. Draft sent to Reinfts School ST VENANT. 2nd Yorks officers returned from leave.	
	11.9.15		Companies paraded as for yesterday.	
	12.9.15		C.O. had R Battalion (Hospital).	
	13.9.15		Battalion was inspected by Colonel Travers commanding 23 Infy Bde.	

Army Form C. 2118.

WAR DIARY
or
INTELLIGENCE SUMMARY.
(Erase heading not required.)

Instructions regarding War Diaries and Intelligence Summaries are contained in F.S. Regs., Part II. and the Staff Manual respectively. Title pages will be prepared in manuscript.

Place	Date	Hour	Summary of Events and Information	Remarks and references to Appendices
LES HAIES BASSES	14.9.15		Companies continue marching and field training. Summary of points above typewritten from 9th Regt — 5 Sept 1915 (see appendix 24th Sept).	
	15.9.15		Companies continuing rifles training. Working party 150 (B Co.) supplies trenches Elbow Farm.	
	16.9.15		Companies continuing rifles training	
	17.9.15		2Lt took attend fees Reconnaissance School.	
	18.9.15		Companies as above	
	19.9.15		Companies as above Church Parade	
	20.9.15		Companies as above. Lt Tait went into Hospital.	
	21.9.15		Companies as above. Maj E.R. King attended a frigate experience	
	22.9.15		Companies as above witnesses interviews with Coy Commanders	
	23.9.15		Orders received for forthcoming operations. Preparing for forthcoming operations.	
	24.9.15		One hundred NCO's trained under Capt & and details	

WAR DIARY
or
INTELLIGENCE SUMMARY.

(Erase heading not required.)

Army Form C. 2118.

Place	Date	Hour	Summary of Events and Information	Remarks and references to Appendices
LES HAIES BASSES	24.9.15		to report to O.C. Home Counties Field Coy R.E. During talent tour in the trenches the Sharpshooters achieve results as follows:—	

```
                        Germans         Periscopes
Lt. C. Ashby              1                 1
L/Sgt Reynolds C.3.      11                13
Gpl Whitworth C.         12                21
Gpl Clark J.              1                 8
Gpl Whitehorn R.          2                 5
Gpl Reynolds J.           4                 8
Gpl Church                6                16
                         ——                ——
                         37                71  periscopes
                          3
                         ——
                         40 Germans
                         ══
```

L/Sgt Reynolds Sniper fire

Killed

L/Sgt Reynolds render demonstrating turning the test took as heavy month.

WAR DIARY
or
INTELLIGENCE SUMMARY

(Erase heading not required.)

Army Form C. 2118

Place	Date	Hour	Summary of Events and Information	Remarks and references to Appendices
LES HATTES PASSES	21	9.15	On the 22nd inst. the C.O. sent in the following recommendations:—	Honours Rewards
			Major LEONARD REGINALD KING. A most loyal & valuable second-in-command. Of his zeal, energy & devotion to duty I cannot speak too highly.	
			Captain SIDNEY CEDRIC MATHEWS SMITH. The only Company Commander who has served in that capacity without a break since we landed here. Thanks to good reliable officer.	
			Captain Adjutant GEOFFREY ARTHUR HOLME BOWER. An admirable Adjutant and never ceased working. He am his utmost throughout the campaign & considers his services worthy of recognition.	MILITARY CROSS
			Captain SYDNEY HAROLD GILLETT. Has repeatedly shown the greatest gallantry by his example has had a most inspiring effect upon all ranks see report of his carrying on his occasion of the 5th V.C. in detail for the 21st Aug. He has already been granted the V.C. I forward his recommendation now of the Y.C. Gillett had however this forward to a D.S.O. as a hand accessory of a D.S.O.	Y.C. or D.S.O.

[signature]

WAR DIARY or INTELLIGENCE SUMMARY

Army Form C. 2118

Place	Date	Hour	Summary of Events and Information	Remarks and references to Appendices
LES HAIES BASSES	24. IX. 15			HONOURS & REWARDS
			Lieut. CECIL ASHBY. Who has organised & trained the Sharpshooters of this Battn. Thanks to his own personal example training he has brought them to a very high standard of efficiency & has been able experimentally to obtain control of the enemy's sharpshooters so largely to reduce the casualties of this Battn. The nature of the work done has necessitated taking risks beyond the ordinary & this Officer was unfortunately wounded on Aug. 21.	
			2/Lieut. THOMAS VERE CHENNELL. This officer has organised & trained the Grenadiers of the Battn. & has done exceptionally good work. He has for a long time past been attached to the Brigade Grenadier School.	
			No 179 A/Cpl. Regt. Sergt. A very good reliable N.C.O. has done excellent Major G.S. work all his time first as Company Sergeant Major BURROCK. lately as Regt. Sergeant Major. His services are worthy of recognition.	D.C.M.

Army Form C. 2118

WAR DIARY
or
INTELLIGENCE SUMMARY
(Erase heading not required.)

Instructions regarding War Diaries and Intelligence Summaries are contained in F.S. Regs., Part II. and the Staff Manual respectively. Title Pages will be prepared in manuscript.

Place	Date	Hour	Summary of Events and Information	Remarks and references to Appendices
LES HAIES BASSES	24.IX.15			Honours & Rewards
			No.780 Sergeant E.J. KING who has been put in command of a Palce every night we have been in the Trenches since we landed in France last March. He has shown himself a most daring & intelligent patrol leader, has frequently brought in valuable information when apparently volunteered for every service of danger that has been open to him. I consider him thoroughly deserving of some recognition. He has returned the thanks of the Divisional Comdr.	D.C.M.
			No.3420 Sergeant W.H. STEWART. As Transport Sergeant has done exceedingly good work.	
			No.625 Pte. W. MOUTRIE. As a stretcher bearer showed the greatest gallantry under heavy fire on May 9th & again on Aug. 25th. brought in wounded men under rifle & machine gun fire for which he received the thanks of the Divisional Commander.	D.C.M.

Army Form C. 2118

WAR DIARY
or
INTELLIGENCE SUMMARY
(Erase heading not required.)

Instructions regarding War Diaries and Intelligence Summaries are contained in F. S. Regs., Part II. and the Staff Manual respectively. Title Pages will be prepared in manuscript.

Place	Date	Hour	Summary of Events and Information	Remarks and references to Appendices
LES HAIES BASSES	24.X.15		No 1133 Pte T.H. FERGUSON. As a stretcher bearer showed the greatest gallantry under heavy fire on Aug 25th — bandaged wounded men under machine gun fire, for which he received the thanks of the Divisional Commander.	Honours Awarded D.C.M.
			No 2334 La.Cpl. A. FULLER. Showed great gallantry resolution & coolness on the night of Aug 25th for which he received the thanks of the Divisional Commander.	
			No 1474 La.Sergt C.F. REYNOLDS. The most daring & successful of our Sharpshooters. They have now succeeded from time to time in shooting a large number of the enemy's snipers thereby saving our own casualties their services are most worthy of recognition.	
			No 1519 Cpl. C.A. WILMOTT. La.Sergt Reynolds has already received the thanks of the Divisional Commander.	

[signature] Capt for Mr

WAR DIARY
or
INTELLIGENCE SUMMARY.
(Erase heading not required.)

Army Form C. 2118

Instructions regarding War Diaries and Intelligence Summaries are contained in F.S. Regs., Part II. and the Staff Manual respectively. Title pages will be prepared in manuscript.

Place	Date	Hour	Summary of Events and Information	Remarks and references to Appendices
LES HAMES BASSES	Sep 21 1915		C.O. returned from Hospital & resumed Command of Battn in the evening. At 7.30 pm the Battn marched off to its position of assembly N.W. of Rouge DE BOUT and there dug itself in during the night.	
ROUGE DE BOUT.	25 Sep 1915		At 4.30 am 3 Battns of 25th I.Bde. assaulted the German trenches in the neighbourhood of LE BRIDOUX penetrating to the 3rd line, capturing 4 Officers and 120 men. The 24th I.Bde., less 1 Battn, was in support along the Rue de la CHAPELLE & the 23rd I.Bde. was in Divisional Reserve along the Rue BACHÉ. The trenches through which the assault of our Battn passed were held by LAMBERT'S detachment consisting of a Battn of the 24th I.Bde. & the 2 Territorial Battns of 26th I.Bde. Soon after midday a German counter attack began to develop & by evening the 25th I.Bde. had withdrawn to our own lines. Our casualties are said to be approximately 1200, and we are said to have inflicted much heavier losses on the enemy and to have captured no objective. Heavy losses on the enemy and to have captured no casualties. Later in the afternoon throughout the night our Battn remained throughout the day in its position of assembly and sustained no casualties. The fire was very heavy & the Battn was withdrawn from the trenches to houses in the neighbourhood.	

Army Form C. 2118.

WAR DIARY
or
INTELLIGENCE SUMMARY.

(Erase heading not required.)

Instructions regarding War Diaries and Intelligence Summaries are contained in F. S. Regs., Part II. and the Staff Manual respectively. Title pages will be prepared in manuscript.

Place	Date	Hour	Summary of Events and Information	Remarks and references to Appendices
ROUGE de BOUT	25th Sept. 1915		The advanced detachments furnished by the Batt were as follows: (a) The 2 Machine Guns & their Crews Bogaes under Bde M Gun Officer at the former Wall. They had one man wounded. (b) The Grenadiers under proportion at the Bde. School were moved to a position of readiness at CROIX MARÉCHAL under 2/Lt Chewter. Though heavily shelled they evaded and no casualties. (c) The party of 100 men under Capt Newland attached to the some Coumine Field Coy. R.E. remained during the day at FLEURBAIX and were employed during the night in repairing the trenches wire in front of our trenches. They had no casualties.	
do	26th Sept. 1915		The Battn assumed its position of Assembly at 4.30 a.m. and remained here during the day returning to the neighbouring billets as before in the evening. We had one man wounded by shrapnel. The 3 detachen parties remained in their positions of yesterday. Captain Marshall's detachment having two men wounded. The Guns were active on both sides during the day. First Line Transport moved up to Le QUESNOY. Today 50 Grands returned from the 6th French Army with the War Dog ATHOS (No 2069)	

[signature] Captain

Army Form C. 2118.

WAR DIARY
or
INTELLIGENCE SUMMARY.
(Erase heading not required.)

Place	Date	Hour	Summary of Events and Information	Remarks and references to Appendices
ROUGE du BOIS.	27 Sept. 1915		The Battn. took up its position of Assembly at 4.30 a.m. and remained here during the day. At 5.30 p.m. it marched to the Rue DAVID and took over from the 5/ Black Watch the trench line between the west end of the Canal Street and the Rue de la BOUTILLERIE, our Coys. being in the trenches in order from right to left: A. C. B. & D. Captain Machardo's detachment remained at FLEURBAIX. The Brigade Machine Guns were withdrawn but did not rejoin the Battn. 2/Lt. Chevallier's Grenadiers remained at CROIX MARECHAL.	
LA BOUTILLERIE	28 Sept. 1915		Grenadier detachment returned to BARRETTE Farm. In the evening we handed over positions H.P. 7 and 9 of H.Q. to 2 Middx. withdrew "B" Coy. to CROIX BLANCHÉ & "D" Coy. to billets at CROIX BLANCHÉ. 2/Lt. Gosling returned to duty from hospital. Transport returned to old lines across the river.	
LA BOUTILLERIE	29 Sept. 1915		The Brigade M. Guns returned to the Battn. were sent to CROIX BLANCHÉ, one gun being placed in post here. News received to-night that 3 French Divisions has broken through last German lines in CHAMPAGNE. Letter received sanctioning further extension of C.O.'s Command of the Battn. for a further period of 2 years from 1st Nov? next	

1577 Wt.W10791/1773 500,000 1/15 D. D. & L. A.D.S.S./Forms/C. 2118.

Army Form C. 2118.

WAR DIARY
or
INTELLIGENCE SUMMARY.
(Erase heading not required.)

Instructions regarding War Diaries and Intelligence Summaries are contained in F. S. Regs., Part II. and the Staff Manual respectively. Title pages will be prepared in manuscript.

Place	Date	Hour	Summary of Events and Information	Remarks and references to Appendices
LA BOUTILLERIE	30 Sept 1915		General HUDSON and General TUSON visited trenches duty from hospital. L. TAIT returned to Sharpshooters (Cpl. WILMOTT) shot one German. News received that French has captured 25,000 prisoners + 100 guns.	

E.H.
Lieut 1/7 Middlesex R (T.F.)

Saint Power
Capt M.
1/7 Middlesex R
(T.F.)

23rd Inf. Bde.
8th Division

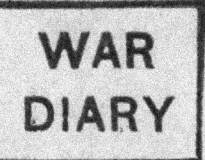

1/7th Battalion

THE MIDDLESEX REGIMENT

AUGUST 1915

Army Form C. 2118.

21/7470

23/8

5th Division

WAR DIARY
or
INTELLIGENCE SUMMARY.
(Erase heading not required.)

Place	Date	Hour	Summary of Events and Information	Remarks and references to Appendices
			CONFIDENTIAL War Diary of 1/7th Middlesex Regt for August 1915 Aug – Sep 15 Vol VI	

Instructions regarding War Diaries and Intelligence Summaries are contained in F. S. Regs., Part II. and the Staff Manual respectively. Title pages will be prepared in manuscript.

WAR DIARY or INTELLIGENCE SUMMARY

Army Form C. 2118.

Place	Date	Hour	Summary of Events and Information	Remarks and references to Appendices
BAC ST MAUR	1.VIII.15		Rest day. Following working parties detailed: Knots towards KEWERLY 15 Pioneers 100 foot prestos 100 ss shovels. 50 men "A" Coy 50 shovels & 25 picks. Khyat CROIX MARECHAL gun. 100 foot sols, Dy. 50 shovels 50 picks. Rheat CROIX BLANCHE gun, 50 men "A" Coy Pothier "Gifted Tram Terminus No 3, 32, 30 picks & 25 shovels.	
	11.VIII.15		Amalgamation of B ... Carried from today 7 Officers and 444 other ranks forming No 1 HQ been DOYLIE & GP. Multivallas day 1 formed the battalion less Officers 2nd Lieut WOODROFFE, P.C. KAY and GEDWARD. Seo men (100 A, 50 A, 50 C) and a working party. Party Hdqts HB002,2 (notrobed).	
	111.VIII.15		Conference at Bn HQ.	
	4.VIII.15		No 9133 Pte DUNCAN having refused to be electrically C.O. on a charge of disobedience of orders was sentenced by a F.G.C.M. to six months imprisonment with hard labour.	
	6.VIII.15		The Brigadier formally inspected the Bath. by Companies. In 6. days Brigadier approved the official announcement in the London Gazette of the bestowale of the Distinguished Conduct Medal on 1027 Lce Sgt F.J. Hocking, 9488 Co (since died of wounds) and 953 Lce Corp W.H. Willis of "A" Co.	

Army Form C. 2118.

WAR DIARY
or
INTELLIGENCE SUMMARY.
(Erase heading not required.)

Instructions regarding War Diaries and Intelligence Summaries are contained in F. S. Regs., Part II. and the Staff Manual respectively. Title pages will be prepared in manuscript.

Place	Date	Hour	Summary of Events and Information	Remarks and references to Appendices
BAC ST MAUR	7 VIII 15		Our Local Class of Instruction for Officers Juniors to-day. The Officers of the 8th Inniskn. returning to their Battn. Recommendations for promotions of officers in the 8th Inniskn. were sent in to-day.	
RUE DU MOULIN	8 VIII 15		The Battn. took over the right half of No 4 Section of the trenches and a part of No 3 Section. 'A' & 'B' Cos with two machine guns holding the trenches. 'C' & 'D' Cos with the other two guns being in Battn. reserve at CROIX BLANCHE.	
	9 VIII 15		7634 Corpl Longwopt Georges Tapkins left for England to-day. L/Sergt. Pendleton of Bomb. was wounded this morning, and Sgt. E. J. King badly wounded in the later, whilst on a working party accompanied by Maj. Genl. Hudson. C.B. C.I.E. Comm. the Division	
	10 VIII 15		Lt. Genl. Sir Genl. Clark inspected the trenches. In the afternoon the enemy first sent gun shells into the convent behind our lines wounding one man. Our snipers got in German to-day.	
	11 VIII 15		2/Lt Macintosh joined the Battn. to-day.	

T2134. Wt. W708—776. 500000. 4/15. Sir J. C. & S.

Army Form C. 2118.

WAR DIARY
or
INTELLIGENCE SUMMARY.
(Erase heading not required.)

Instructions regarding War Diaries and Intelligence Summaries are contained in F.S. Regs., Part II. and the Staff Manual respectively. Title pages will be prepared in manuscript.

Place	Date	Hour	Summary of Events and Information	Remarks and references to Appendices
RUE DU MOULIN (COY.)	12.VIII.15		Our snipers shot two Germans to-day. A report was received that from the French Sniper School that Sgt. Bennet 'A' Co. had been badly wounded.	
	13.VIII.15		Pts Mitchell 'A' Co. and Watson 'B' Co. were killed to-day. Our snipers accounted for one German to-day and Williamson return from Sniper. A Machine Gun was put out of action by a rifle shot on the breach casing.	
	14.VIII.15		Lce.Corp. Benson 'D' Co. was killed on a working party. Our snipers accounted for three of the enemy. 8th Division Horse Show was held at SAILLY. Major L.R King went to Hospital.	
	15.VIII.15		Conference of Commanding Officers at Bde. Hd.Qrs at 10.0 am. Snipers accounted for 3 Germans during the day. LtWard returned from hospital.	
	16.VIII.15		'C' and 'D' Coys relieved 'A' and 'B' Coys in the trenches to-day the latter going into Bde Reserve at CROIX BLANCHE. Snipers accounted for one German to-day.	
	17.VIII.15		All quiet in the trenches. Our snipers shot one German	

Army Form C. 2118.

WAR DIARY
or
INTELLIGENCE SUMMARY.
(Erase heading not required.)

Instructions regarding War Diaries and Intelligence Summaries are contained in F. S. Regs., Part II. and the Staff Manual respectively. Title pages will be prepared in manuscript.

Place	Date	Hour	Summary of Events and Information	Remarks and references to Appendices
RUE DU MOULIN	18/VIII/15		The two Coys in the trenches were relieved by the Black Watch and the 1st Worcesters during the afternoon, and took over in exchange 3 Q and Half 3 R from the Scottish Rifles. At the same time two sections of 'A' Co relieved the Scottish Rifles in MILL ROAD Post and a Machine Gun and team were withdrawn from the trenches to the same post. During the day our snipers picked off some Germans.	
	19/VIII/15		During the morning General Clark visited the Gen. At 3pm the two sections of 'A' Co were withdrawn from MILL ROAD Post to CROIX BLANCHE and replaced by a platoon of 'D' Coy from the trenches. 2/Lt K.C. Moore and 50 King went on leave to-day. A Central Post was yesterday established at CROIX BLANCHE drawn from 'B' Co, to prevent horses + transport passing South of that point between the hours of 4.0 am and 8.0 pm.	
	20/VIII/15		General Hudson, commanding the Division, inspected the trenches	

Army Form C. 2118.

WAR DIARY
or
INTELLIGENCE SUMMARY.
(Erase heading not required.)

Instructions regarding War Diaries and Intelligence Summaries are contained in F.S. Regs., Part II. and the Staff Manual respectively. Title pages will be prepared in manuscript.

Place	Date	Hour	Summary of Events and Information	Remarks and references to Appendices
RUE DU MOULIN	20.VIII.15 (cont)		During the night a demonstration was made by one of the Indian Divisions a little to the South of our sector.	
	21.VIII.15		Maj L.R. King returns from hospital. The snipers succeeded in shooting two Germans, but Lt C Ashby, in charge of our snipers was wounded.	
	22.VIII.15		Lt Challen was put in charge of the snipers and succeeded in shooting one German.	
	23.VIII.15		Conference of Commanding Officers at Bot. Hd Qrs in the morning arrange to begin work to-night on new scheme of defences. In the evening "C" + "D" Coys were relieved in the trenches by A + B Coys. Afternoon "C" + "D" Coys went into billets at CROIX BLANCHE in Brigade Reserve.	
Rue du Bois	26.VIII.15	3.15 pm	Battn H.Q. moved back to Rue Reserve in Rue du BOIS. The snipers observed a number of offensive little villages behind the trenches. They shot 4 Germans. Must have lost others as only 3 men away. The General sent a signaller by wireless	

Army Form C. 2118

WAR DIARY
or
INTELLIGENCE SUMMARY
(Erase heading not required.)

Place	Date	Hour	Summary of Events and Information	Remarks and references to Appendices
Rue du Bois	25.VIII.15		During the night a Patrol came into contact with the enemy of which the details are embodied in the following official Report.	

Report on action of Patrol night 25/2 6 Aug/15.

At 10 p.m. on night of 25th a patrol of 22 [Gloucesters] was sent out by Capt. Gillett with instructions to cover. The party working in front of the trench. The patrol was warned not to go too far forward because of the bright moonlight. The patrol advanced towards the German lines, the Officer & 2 men leading, the remainder following 10 paces in rear. They advanced to about 80 yards from the German parapet, keeping 100 yards [distance?] to the left of our advance trench N.11 at 3.6. At this point they appear to have come unexpectedly upon another party of [illegible] his two [illegible] opened fire killing the Officer & 1 man of the advance party, wounding another, the remainder was killed (No.23/2 Pte Short) as he who shot evidently saw [illegible]

WAR DIARY
or
INTELLIGENCE SUMMARY

Army Form C. 2118

(Erase heading not required.)

Place	Date	Hour	Summary of Events and Information	Remarks and references to Appendices
Quadra	RMS 25.VIII.15		(Cont.) enemy as he hurled about into the dug outs. There taking effect on all this covered was not reopened for some minutes. The evacuation of fire saved the rear party which were able to drop into a ditch under cover. No. 2334 Sergt Fuller A. at once went back to rejoin & take leave. Meanwhile Capt Gillett having the front of fire to shoot. He helped him the wounded man reach & get into our own No.6x.No.9 mouters to rejoin to Capt where he was afterwards joined by the stretcher bearers & took charge. Under Sgt. his directions the bodies of the wounded were carried. 2.Lt Godward top another two who were knocked afterwards bounced were received throughout under heavy fire. Capt Gillett got out to custody of Sgt. Gilbert but they were unable to bring it in owing to heavy rifle fire and to the Germans having cut of them. Further instruction taken. Capt Gillett	

Army Form C 2118

WAR DIARY
or
INTELLIGENCE SUMMARY
(Erase heading not required.)

Instructions regarding War Diaries and Intelligence Summaries are contained in F.S. Regs., Part II. and the Staff Manual respectively. Title Pages will be prepared in manuscript.

Place	Date	Hour	Summary of Events and Information	Remarks and references to Appendices
Rue de Bois	25.VIII.15		cont. personally covered the retirement of the stretcher bearers and the remainder of the patrol and in my opinion displayed a coolness and gallantry worthy of the highest commendation.	
do	26.VIII.15		The Snipers shot 3 Germans today. The following is commendation forwarded to the Brigadier General for consideration. 2nd Lieut. Ashby who has organised and trained the sharpshooters of this Battalion, mainly by his own personal example and daring he has brought them to a very high standard of efficiency and has been able systematically to obtain control of the enemy's sharpshooters & so largely to reduce the casualties of this Battalion. The nature of the work done has necessitated taking risks beyond the ordinary and this Officer was unfortunately wounded on Aug. 15.15. No 70. Sgt. E. Thing. This NCO has been out reconnoitring the hostile trenches practically every night returning in without a scratch.	

WAR DIARY or INTELLIGENCE SUMMARY

Army Form C. 2118

Place	Date	Hour	Summary of Events and Information	Remarks and references to Appendices
Rue du Bois	27.VIII.15		Since our arrival in France that march, Hulluch shown highly a most daring and intelligent patrol leader, has frequently brought back information that he had systematically unlimited for our service at large. He has been often taken under his thoroughly knowing ground recognition. NOTE: 4. A/Sgt C. F. Reynolds. The most daring and successful of our Sharp-shooters. He had most successful from time to time in shooting a large number of the enemy. Sharpshooters though necessary our own casualties. His services are of greatest value and cannot be [...]	
do	28.VIII.15		Snipers shot 2 Germans exchanges. 3 periscopes & telescopic sights destroyed. 2nd Lt Godwin & men returned to their general. However commander of 8th Divn was called to this morning. There is a considerable matter to also general Capt Gillett's conduct on the 25th. Strongly recommending a recovery of VC. A Company Officer, report [...] reported the transport of battalion. Snipers shot 2 Germans and smashed four periscopes.	
do	29.VIII.15		A message was received that Snipers [...] and [...] station that an information had been received of an attack in the front. Snipers inflicted no casualties as Germans smashed periscopes.	

WAR DIARY or INTELLIGENCE SUMMARY

Army Form C. 2118

(Erase heading not required.)

Place	Date	Hour	Summary of Events and Information	Remarks and references to Appendices
Rehan B.H.S.	30.VIII.15		Conference G.O.C.'s at Brigade H.Q. 10.a.m.	

A.D.M.S. report of the Divisional Commander for further details regarding the patrol of the 25th Aug. O.C. furnishes the following to latch'd Bearers & following information. The list of the patrol under detachment is as follows —

No 2334 Sergt. Fuller a.
" 1733 Pte. Prevost. C. H. } R.A.M.C. ambulance.
" 2586 " Price. B.
" 1560 " Hilton. C. L.
" 2487 " Cabin. F.
" 2262 " Gilbert. T.W.

No. 2334 Sergt. Fuller's comment is "I think that in spite of quite a snow as he could get the patrol under cover, he went back for stretcher bearers & carried two to hospital. He then assisted to carry a wounded stretcher bearer's body back to trenches. He again returned and assisted the stretcher bearers to take back Pte Woods."

All the men showed very keen fire.

Particulars of stretcher bearers are as follows: —

No. 295 Sergt Nash. W. F.
" 1354 Pvt. Brown. C. H. } carriers but Pte Price.
" 1560 Pte. Hilton. C. L.
" 1053 Anstruther. B. } carried but Pte Johnson.
" 190 Pte Morton. N.

Place	Date	Hour	Summary of Events and Information	Remarks and references to Appendices
Rue des Bois	30.VIII.15			

No 625 Promontier M.
1133 2nd Fergusson T.H. } carried out Pr.Mord

The two following stations shown are particularly worthy of note of those having *humanly* mentioned for gallant conduct in the action against FROMELLES on 9th Sept last. No 625 Promontier M. who was noted in my original report followed Capt. Gilbert and seriously, it was rendered something he was wrong, having endeavour to carry the body of 2nd Lieut Boynard who returned the ritualto to carry trench Pathord
No. 1133 2nd Lieut Fergusson who with Capt.Gilbert made a determined effort to get back the body of the gallant Lieut. but was unable to do so by heavy rifle fire. He then made his way back from PtwMord back to the trenches. To attack the report of Capt.Laville whose the Senior Capt. in the Battalion therefore herein to Capt.Gilbert Capt.In his Report

Between 10.30 and 11 pm I saw scented on the top of the parapet talking to Capt.Gilbert to Capt.Gilbert key men of his party. I heard the cry of the shells from this and man of the patrol on which Capt.Gilbert with others the afterwards learnt was Promontier, rushed rapidly away in the direction from

WAR DIARY or INTELLIGENCE SUMMARY

Army Form C.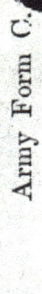

Place	Date	Hour	Summary of Events and Information	Remarks and references to Appendices
Quadrm Bois	30.VIII.15		which the wound came. I afterwards saw the bodies of 2 Lt Graham & the two wounded men brought in climbing towards the front. I conclude the Germans by the flashes of their rifles had seen down Machine Gun fire from their Sap-head & destroy the Patrol. We could not fire on them for fear of hitting our own patrol. Shortly afterwards Cpl Hunt accompanied by Pte Cooper returned to the trenches. We totalled 3 Killed such Patrol and on the stretchers. We are however heavy rifle fire most of the time. This is all that Lieut Grey Cumming, Cpl Hughes, Sholve, Germain and smoker Gumbeyer.	
	31.VIII.15		About 5.20 p.m. the Germans exploded a mine in front of the Devons & afterwards shelled their trenches. Our Batty replied. Pte Gorn (Machine Gunner) was hit whilst waiting. The Airplane shot by Germans. Thanks to Knipples.	

S.C.T.
2nd Lt
Commanding B Company R
Lordon
F. Coyte Att
H Machl

23rd Inf. Bde
8th Division

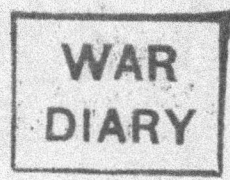

1/7th Battalion,

THE MIDDLESEX REGIMENT

JULY 1915

121/6539

8th Battalion

4/7 Hampshire

Vol I

From 1st to 31st July 1915.

Army Form C. 2118

WAR DIARY
or
INTELLIGENCE SUMMARY
(Erase heading not required.)

War Diary of
1/7th Bn. Middlesex Regt
from 1st July 1915
to 31st July 1915.

Bonguenine

WAR DIARY or INTELLIGENCE SUMMARY

Army Form C. 2118.

Place	Date	Hour	Summary of Events and Information	Remarks and references to Appendices
LA HOUTLERE	1.7.15		The Battalion took out Nº 4 section of trench from 2 Rifle Bde to the left half of Nº 3 section from 1st London Rgt. Three coys held the trench line in order from right Coys B, C, D. A Co was held in support in billets at Rue DAVID with one platoon divided between posts 3a and 4a.	
do	2.7.14.15		At 10 a.m. Sgt Jones D Coy crawled out through boxwire & killed a German about 20 yds out and a brought in rifle & equipment. Boxwire left in place. German Rgt [crossed out] — During the day garrisons holding 3a were withdrawn in accordance with instructions from the Brigade.	
do	3.7.14.15		Quiet. No man wounded.	
do	4.7.14.15		Quiet. No. Pte Stanch "D" Co killed & 2¹⁰ W.C. Cosgrove severely wounded.	
do	5.7.14.15		No 9558 L/Cpl Smith wounded.	
do	6.7.14.15		Quiet. One man wounded.	
do	7.7.14.15		Quiet. Battalion was relieved by 2 Scottish Rifles and went into billets	
RUE DE BRUGES			along Rue de BRUGES in Divisional Reserve. The total casualties during tour were 2 killed & 7 wounded. 9th [illegible] Bn. 7th L/Cpl Robertson 7th L/Cpl [illegible]	

Army Form C. 2118.

WAR DIARY
or
INTELLIGENCE SUMMARY.
(Erase heading not required.)

Place	Date	Hour	Summary of Events and Information	Remarks and references to Appendices
Rue du BRUGES	8.VII.15		Lts Birkbeck & Ashby rejoined for duty. A working party of 200 men was furnished to 175 Field Coy R.E. for work at LA BOUTILLERIE and a working party of 100 men from B Coy for work at LA CORDONNERIE. A draft of 40 men of F. Hursts arrived this day all being from Hospital.	
do	9.VII.15		Col Bott T.T., V.D. Hon Col 5th Manch visited the Battalion. Two working parties each of 100 men furnished by C Coy for work under 15 Field Coy R.E. in rear of Nos 2 & 3 sections.	(BD'Coys)
do	10.VII.15		Lt A.J. Gliphis rejoined from Hospital. One working party of 200 men provided for work under 15 Field Coy R.E. for work in rear of No 2 Section	(B'& D' Coys)
do	11.VII.15		A working party of 200 men (B' & D' Coys) were provided for work under 15 Field Coy R.E. for work in rear of No 2 Section.	
do	12.VII.15		A working party of 100 men (A Coy) was provided for work under 15 Field Coy R.E. at CROIX MARECHAL, a party of 50 men (A Coy) found under 15-79 Coy R.E. at CROIX BLANCHE redoubt, 50 men (A & C Coys) for work under 15-79 Coy R.E. at Trenches	N363.2

Army Form C. 2118.

WAR DIARY
or
INTELLIGENCE SUMMARY.
(Erase heading not required.)

Place	Date	Hour	Summary of Events and Information	Remarks and references to Appendices
Rue de BRUGES	13.VII.15		The Battalion went into No 1. Brigade Reserve area taking over Billets round CROIX BLANCHE & CROIX MARECHAL from 2 Rivers. A Cy. Hd.Quarters & Coy. at Croix MARECHAL, D Cy at CROIX BLANCHE. No. 3 Platoon (2 Lt.J. Awning) garrisoned post 27 & No 4 Platoon (Lt Shipton) post 26.	
do	14.VII.15.		A working party was detailed of 150 men "C" Cy. & 50 men "B" Cy. reported at Great South Trawl Shed N.3 & 3.2 for work under 15th Field Coy R.E.	
do	15.VII.15.		The working party detailed for last night paraded this night under Capt Chitty. The Commanding Officer Capt. S.H. Gillett proceeded to England on 7 days leave.	
do	16.VII.15		2 Lt Levy went into Hospital. A working party of 50 men from D Coy was provided to work under Lt Newhouse 15 Fd. Coy R.E. near LA CORDONNERIE and 150 of "C" Cy. & worked under Lt Lambert 15 Fd. Coy R.E. also near LA CORDONNERIE.	

Army Form C. 2118.

WAR DIARY
or
INTELLIGENCE SUMMARY.
(Erase heading not required.)

Place	Date	Hour	Summary of Events and Information	Remarks and references to Appendices
	17.VII.15		2Lt C. C. Sherlock reported for duty. A working party of 50 men from "B" Coy was provided tomorrow. 1st NEWHOUSE 15 Field Company R.E. 4150 from "A" Coy tomorrow under 1st LAMBERT 15 Field Company R.E. at LA CORDONNERIE.	
	18.VII.15		Major L. R. King attended a conference at Bde H.Q. A working party of 50 men from "B" Coy was provided tomorrow under Sgt. GODDARD 15 D. Coy R.E. 4150 from "C" Coy tomorrow under Lt LAMBERT 15 Field Coy R.E. at LA CORDONNERIE.	
	19.7.15		The Battn. relieved the 2 M.R. in left half of No. 3. section & the whole of No. 4. section.	
	20.7.15		All quiet in trenches. No. 1141 Sgt. H.T. KNOWERS killed at Sharpshooters post in ConventWalk & one man wounded.	
	21.7.15		All quiet in trenches	
	22.7.15		All quiet in trenches, one man wounded. 3 officers 3/7 Mx & 6 others 3/8 Mx not reported for duty & a draft of 40 men. 2Lts A.R. Hopkins, Adamson, G.E., & Nesbory, N.H., 3/8 Mx. Ht & Lt Thursdon, A., 2 Lts Eastman, L.W., Routh, C.F.R., Nevin, Ryan, A.C. Jr., Jones, P.R.B. and Bailey, S.V. of 3/7 Mx & Knicker.	

1577 Wt. W10791/1773 500,000 1/15 D. D. & L. A.D.S.S./Forms/C. 2118.

Army Form C. 2118.

WAR DIARY
or
INTELLIGENCE SUMMARY.
(Erase heading not required.)

Place	Date	Hour	Summary of Events and Information	Remarks and references to Appendices
	23.VII.15		C.O. returned from leave previous Command; C.O. Hill attendance from leave.	
	24.VII.15		All Spirit Professors Wells, Ph. Day, des	
	25.VII.15		Conference at Bn HQ at 10.30am all sap'rs together memoranda handed over by D Section during evening, twenty two no Bayonne reserve along Rue du QVESNEL, 'C' Coy today Dublin hole Nos 21 & 22 with 12 up to on earth & 23 with up latrine.	
	26.7.15		Report of being too near putting in years (2Lts TREMLETT, LACEY, BYHAM & NADDHAMS) received this day. Rapid Ring instructions by SSGT GODDARD 15 Fd Coy RE. Working Party of 200 furnished by A Coy trench mortar, 15 Fd Coy RE + working party of 200 furnished by D Coy trench under Lt GURNEY 15 Field Coy R.E.	
	27.7.15		Made a clean puncture day trip 2+12 inside clay. LR Kay Rathlin	

WAR DIARY or INTELLIGENCE SUMMARY

Place	Date	Hour	Summary of Events and Information	Remarks and references to Appendices
Rue du QUESNES	27.viii.15		Working parties as usual were provided. 7 NCOs & men "C" Coy to workmen Lt GIRNEY 15 & ½ Coy R.E. near CROIX MARECHAL. 100 men & 1 sgt to Gey — do — 50 men "C" Coy workmen Lt LAMBERT 15th A Coy R.E. near Fromelines N3 B3 ½. 30 men "D" Coy — do —	
do	28.viii.15		Nothing of importance. Nothing particular to report or under. 1 man A. of man C Cy been killed.	
			100 men "C" Coy workmen Lt WENHOUSE 15 A. Coy R.E. near CROIX BLANCHE. 150 men "A" Coy do Lt STONE do near CROIX MARECHAL 100 men "B" Coy do do do 50 men A & D Coy do do do	
do	29.viii.15		Commanding Officer took part Officers recoennes in return to England's trenches tomorrow.	
			100 men "A" Coy provided work under Lt LAMBERT 15 Fd. Coy R.E. near Fromelines N3 B3 ½ 150 men "D" Coy do do Lt GURNEY do near CROIX MARECHAL 75 mm Bcoy do do 75 mm Ccoy do do	
do	30.viii.15		Capt BUCKLAND & 2 Lt REYNOLDS reports to duty from 2 of minor operators. A separate return of reserve was forwarded today. Lt SCOTT and attached to 1) Cy. 150 men A & B Coys workmen Lt NEWHOUSE 15 Fd Coy R.E. near CROIX BLANCHE 50 mm A B Coy do do	

WAR DIARY
or
INTELLIGENCE SUMMARY.

Army Form C. 2118.

Place	Date	Hour	Summary of Events and Information	Remarks and references to Appendices
Rue du QUESNES	31.VII.15		Draft of 3 officers 111 other ranks arrived from Grantham into billets N°P.R. LYS. Distributed Divisional Reserve Hd qr R.Cp. AMESMAR 'C'Cp. PORT A CLOUS. 'A'& 'B'Cps on the NATHA & E.M Bns at Port Rouge. The following is a copy of a letter received from 8th Div through 23rd Inf.Bde. : a copy has been sent to R.O. Grantham. 8 Div No 59/33 (A). Head quarters. 23 July 1915. I am directed by the G.O.C. 8th Division to request that you will convey to No. 955 L/Cpl W.H. Willis 17th Battn. Middlesex Regt, his appreciation of the N.C.O's courage & knowledge of the patrol when he attacked a German section with bombs. Another became a prisoner of his action. (Signed) F. D. Logan Major D.A.A. & Q.M.G. 8th Division	

23 Inf. Bde.
8th Division

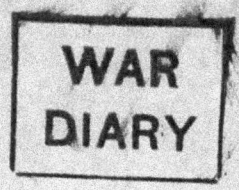

1/7th Battalion

The Middlesex Regiment

June 1915

8th Division

Note: Batt. absorbed 48 Middlesex 23.6.15.
the latter running independent
formation 2.8.15

12/6529

17th Middlesex
Vol IV
From 1st 6 30th June 1915

Battalion absorbed
m 23 6's.

Army Form C. 2118.

WAR DIARY
or
INTELLIGENCE SUMMARY.

(Erase heading not required.)

Instructions regarding War Diaries and Intelligence Summaries are contained in F.S. Regs., Part II. and the Staff Manual respectively. Title pages will be prepared in manuscript.

Place	Date	Hour	Summary of Events and Information	Remarks and references to Appendices

Confidential

War Diary of.

14th Machine Regt.

from 1st June 1915
to 30th June 1915.

WAR DIARY
or
INTELLIGENCE SUMMARY.

Army Form C. 2118

Place	Date	Hour	Summary of Events and Information	Remarks and references to Appendices
WANGERIE	1.6.15		Nothing to Report.	
do	2.VI.15		Returned to E. lines relieving the 2.14th there. Companies in order from Right Regt. C, D, A & B. Two platoons each from C, D & B Coys were held back for supporting posts. Two machine guns were taken over from 2.14th that giving 4 in the line.	
FAUQUISSART	3.VI.15		French lines have readjusted the Rifle pits taking over our right Coy thus necessitating their own boundary between LE lines. to be at the same time as the boundary between right Coy & 2 Sco. Rifles which was occupied by C. Coy. Our machine gun was also now Replaced in Redoubt E1 and C. Coy was re-enforced by 2 sections from test post.	No1676.
do	4.VI.15		Spr Young A.S.I.G. was killed at 9 hrs evening and Stewart mortar shells with W/Pty howling 7 men. Telephone Pts fr Artillery informals, (invited) so had they sent down & rest work into R.F.a lines from LAVENTIE which arrived at midnight. Stores Estella wife (German lines) Germans replied with dugouts Mopsticks of from Sunday orders from the answered with	

WAR DIARY
or
INTELLIGENCE SUMMARY.
(Erase heading not required.)

Army Form C. 2118.

Place	Date	Hour	Summary of Events and Information	Remarks and references to Appendices
FAVUISSART	4.VI.15		Orders received not to fire again unless Enemy fired first, then Bfd 2 shells for every one of theirs.	
do	5.VI.15		Enemy bombarded H.5 trenches E.1 from 7.30 – 8.30 am & again from 9–10 am & half the lines were destroyed. Two men were killed. Capt Gregory Rance Lt Tait and 5 men wounded. H.Q. here in consequence transferred to Post 11.	
do	6.VI.15		Trenches wet & transport very difficult. Lt Fry R.A.M.C. to Ambulance Jones today. Capt Rowe returns from leave. Starts over duties of Adjutant. Bomb'd intermittent. Saw quiet in trenches. Three killed, wounded 6.	
do	7.VI.15		All quiet in trenches. Four men wounded. Capt Howard & Lt Lancaster Lgt sent into trenches for 4 days instruction.	
do	8.VI.15		All quiet in trenches. 3 men wounded. Battalion was relieved in evening by 2 Middx Regt in supporting coys 2 Ryl Berks 2nd in WANGERIE. A Coy in supporting Coy, B Coy in billets. Posts 11, 12, 13, C & D Coys in billets. The 6 days in trenches 3 Killed and 28 wounded.	
WANGERIE	9.VI.15		Battn attended Divisional Baths at SAILLY and formed two coys. Working parties on under 5 Coy to S.R. N2, C.8.2 at 9.30 pm from under 1 Pt in C1 & ORE also 2nd Pt, Coy D.E. Creosote 1/12 C.2.0 at 9.0 pm	

Army Form C. 2118.

WAR DIARY
or
INTELLIGENCE SUMMARY.
(Erase heading not required.)

Instructions regarding War Diaries and Intelligence Summaries are contained in F. S. Regs., Part II. and the Staff Manual respectively. Title pages will be prepared in manuscript.

Place	Date	Hour	Summary of Events and Information	Remarks and references to Appendices
NANGERIE	10.VI.15.		Nothing to record. No notices two killed Serg in morning with wiring party at Rue PE TILLOY. Working party as under was furnished from nine. 2/3rds Canterburys apstay at Post depot M17 a S16. at 2 o'clock two months & 2 Lieutenants. 20 Canterburys names — 28 men C 5/5 30 — A 5/5 28 — B 5	
do	11.VI.15		Nothing to record. Working party as under was furnished from nine. 2/Lt Wilkinson 2/Lt R.E. Scott. 50 men C Coy 50 men D Coy Reporting at M12 G.2.0 at 9 pm	
do	12.VI.15		Nothing to record.	
do	13.& 14.VI.15.		Orders received of midday intimating 2 Mx in trenches tomorrow. At 7pm orders received regarding operations to take place on the 15" & 16". At 10.40 pm message received saying men (to be in from 2 M.X trenches by. At 10.50 pm message received that Canterburys on our inner right would be advanced by one day. Reserve orders concerning day's operations received at 7.45am message to men stating that firm seniorite knew up battles of trenches. A further 10 min Reinforcement for the fatigues at Fort No 13. Attyprus 10 min Reinforcement from the fatigues.	
do	14.VI.15			

WAR DIARY
or
INTELLIGENCE SUMMARY.
(Erase heading not required.)

Army Form C. 2118.

Place	Date	Hour	Summary of Events and Information	Remarks and references to Appendices
WANGERIE	6.VI.15		Forty lines. At 9 p.m. bombarded enemy's trenches lasting 1/2 an hour. At about 10.30 p.m. transport of brigade passed. At 11 p.m. outskirts bombarded. Was enemy trenches into which the entrenchments appeared apparently of 4 H.M. bombardment. Heavy activity for the 9 p.m. 11 p.m. bombardment.	
do	15.VI.15		Further bombardments took place at 1 a.m. 3 a.m. 4 a.m. ending on my alight response from the enemy guns. C & D Coys were told in trenches. Several attempts by patrols to take not obtained. At 9 p.m. relieved 2 H× in E. lines having 2 men wounded in doing so. 2 lifted stretchers hospital acct. influenza.	
FAUQUISSART	16.VI.15		All quiet in trenches. 3 men wounded	
do	17.VI.15		Kopt[?]ing (arm'd decreased) enemy life in, to 4 & 4 loft riflemen in trenches reinforcing we preparing to distinguish ourselves inclined. At about 6 p.m. enemy fried 2 french mortar shells wounding one man. Called for our Artillery to respond sent for [?] into trenches from L'MENTIE which came about 7 p.m.	
do	18.VI.15		Received news that remains of 11th Middx met in ambulance ant the half [?]. Slipper 6.0 & 7.0 pm at Laventie [?] took place. Right [?] who received casualty 2 I/C 4th [?] buried to the [?] hospital with acquired cough.	

WAR DIARY or INTELLIGENCE SUMMARY

Army Form C. 2118

Place	Date	Hour	Summary of Events and Information	Remarks and references to Appendices
FAUQUISSART	19.VI.15		During the morning an hour daylight No 27. S.O.S. was forwarded on through telephone to the German cab lines and received the Reg Hand short Dugouts in front of our stations which in safety. The brigades but the camouflage to hide donkey the supply to had men attd shelling our men being killed. The wounded afternoon. Report No 15 attaché kilometer K21 g 22 h 6th. Battalion togged & to 15th dated 18th June. Casualty	G.B.G.
do	20.VI.15		During the night reports of events, No 955. League Republic advanced of the Germans of there are there absence of the hundred over the trenches into the German front line. They returned atter failure without casualties. At the same time No 730. S.O.S. S.O.S. flying with two some atb men the was German Stripes as new Rue D'ENFER and two attempt made to occupy to twenty yards. The work and two to make use returned from Rue D'ENFER without success	
do	21.VI.15		During the night S.O.S. again but reports into the German advance trench finding it unoccupied. Admiring the remains of the Germans killed widening 9 grave + 409 arrivals	

WAR DIARY or INTELLIGENCE SUMMARY

Army Form C. 2118.

Place	Date	Hour	Summary of Events and Information	Remarks and references to Appendices
FLAMERTINGHE	21.VI.15		Major E.D.W. Gregory arrived at SALLY Station from neighbourhood of POPERINGHE and went into billets near ROYAL ARTOIS. At 9pm Lt. Stewart Cd. Commanding 10th Northumberland Fusiliers joined the Battalion for instructions.	
do	22.VI.15		During the night Sapper E. Jagoe led attached into the German advanced trenches and received a considerable length of their wire. At daybreak it was perceived that they had placed two new flags in front of their top. Near to Pte Skinner "A" Coy ran out under fire and brought them in. At midday the C.O. attended a conference at Divisional H.Q. concerning the amalgamation of the 8th but when the measures he proposed to impress were approved, he in the evening the Battalion was relieved in the trenches the R. Irish Rifles taking over E1, the 1st London E2, and the 2nd Middlesex remainder. The Bn'r went into billets in Bn reserve in neighbourhood of VAN GERIE. D.C.s to occupying posts 11, 12 & 13. Capt Grey Ragnar returned to the Battalion, & Greig Raw...	

1577 Wt. W1073/1773 500,000 1/15 D.D.&L. A.D.S.S./Forms/C. 2118. 2/15 Rosary & Moris

Place	Date	Hour	Summary of Events and Information	Remarks and references to Appendices
NANGERIE	23.VI.15		The new recruits of the 6 hrs were amalgamated with the Battalion. 2nd/3rd. Eff. Nur., Soi. Officers and 394 men being incorporated. Ambulance 3 Officers and 15 other ranks being detailed to proceed to the Base. Remainder to join 5th Reserve ambulance to their respective Corps. Capt Cripps in [orders] to command "C" Coy and each Platoon of the 5 [sections] sent to corresponding Platoon of the 7th.	
do	24.VI.15		Col Stewart C.B. having completed his period [of] secondment to England, returned [to service] to his information Division to be transferred to 3rd Corps.	
do	25.VI.15		Nothing of [note].	
do	26.VI.15		Lt. & 27. Detach. proceed to duty	8th
do	27.VI.15		Nothing of [note]. [Arrived] at B.A.C. S.T.M.A.V.R. Horsey, Br. Gen. J.E. Aruole accrued command of 23 Inf Bde nie Maj Gen R.T. Hunny Kelpah	
BAC ST MAUR	28.VI.15		Nothing to [report].	
do	29.VI.15		Maj. [T.] R. King [Hospital] and with ambulance. Lt. G.A. Tait [...]	

Army Form C.118.

WAR DIARY
or
INTELLIGENCE SUMMARY.
(Erase heading not required.)

Instructions regarding War Diaries and Intelligence Summaries are contained in F.S. Regs., Part II. and the Staff Manual respectively. Title pages will be prepared in manuscript.

Place	Date	Hour	Summary of Events and Information	Remarks and references to Appendices
BAC ST MAUR	30.VI.15		C.O. representative officers visited the trenches at LA BOUTILLERIE no raiders took over the following day	

[signatures]

23rd Inf. Bde
8th Division

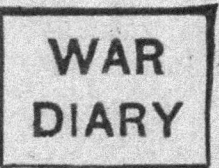

1/7th Battalion

THE MIDDLESEX REGIMENT

MAY 1915.

121/58/25

23
―――
S/d Duvoism

1/7 to Sridillera
―――――――
Vol III 1 — 31.5.157

Army Form C. 2118.

WAR DIARY
or
INTELLIGENCE SUMMARY.

(Erase heading not required.)

Instructions regarding War Diaries and Intelligence Summaries are contained in F. S. Regs., Part II. and the Staff Manual respectively. Title pages will be prepared in manuscript.

Place	Date	Hour	Summary of Events and Information	Remarks and references to Appendices

CONFIDENTIAL

War Diary of
1/7th Middlesex Regt.
from 1st May 1915 to 31st May 1915.

WAR DIARY
or
INTELLIGENCE SUMMARY.

Army Form C. 2118.

Place	Date	Hour	Summary of Events and Information	Remarks and references to Appendices
LE CROSEOBEAU	1 May 19/15		At 7 a.m. orders received to stand firm and be prepared to move at a moment's notice. At 8.30 a.m. orders received to stand down but remain in a state of readiness. At 11 a.m. orders received that normal conditions might be resumed. At 3 p.m. the C.O. received orders for transport to move from SAILLY to H.Q. At 5.30 p.m. orders received to be prepared to move to ESTAIRES and LA GORGUE tomorrow morning. 2/Lt F.D. Smith admitted to hospital with a strained ankle.	
do	2.V.15		The Battalion marched at 2.30 p.m. for LA GORGUE and went into billets there (along the Rue GENDARMERIE and main street. At 2.30 p.m. orders received to take over centre portion of C. & D. lines tomorrow night. At 5.30 p.m. C.O. attended a brigade conference. Lt. H.K. King went into hospital with Asthma.	
LA GORGUE	3.V.15		At 7 a.m. Coy. and Sub. Comd. BACQUEROT Highway and went over new lines. At 1.15 p.m. received fresh orders cancelling the proposed move and instructing us to remain in our present billets until further orders.	
do	4.V.15		The Battalion received orders at 7 a.m. to take over new billets in the	

Army Form C. 2118.

WAR DIARY
or
INTELLIGENCE SUMMARY.

(Erase heading not required.)

Instructions regarding War Diaries and Intelligence Summaries are contained in F. S. Regs., Part II. and the Staff Manual respectively. Title pages will be prepared in manuscript.

Place	Date	Hour	Summary of Events and Information	Remarks and references to Appendices
Rue du Bois.	5.V.15		Rue du Bois 1, 2 Coys. ftn. in support of No1. section of trenches the remainder in support of No 2 section. The path mended.	
		6.10 pm	HofS Coy being placed in support of No 1. section.	
			Coy attended a conference at Bde HQ at 5pm in for the coming operations. The following working parties were provided.	
			2 platoons D Coy at 2.30 pm HQ. No 2 section 2/Scottish Rifles for construction of shelter trench	
			2 platoons C Coy at 5 pm do	
			2 platoons C Coy at 7.30 pm do	
			2 platoons D Coy at 9.30 pm do	
			100 men A Coy reported at Rue du Bois crossroads (N. 2 c 6. 2) at 9.0 pm for work under 1st Honorable's Litters R.E.	
			1 platoon B Coy at about 9.30 pm heavy ammunition	
			1 platoon B Coy at 12 midnight 5/3 way, fourth Seaforth	
			1 platoon B Coy at 2 am 6 hour Rifles to trenches of No 1 section	

Army Form C. 2118.

WAR DIARY
or
INTELLIGENCE SUMMARY.
(Erase heading not required.)

Instructions regarding War Diaries and Intelligence Summaries are contained in F.S. Regs., Part II. and the Staff Manual respectively. Title pages will be prepared in manuscript.

Place	Date	Hour	Summary of Events and Information	Remarks and references to Appendices
	6.V.15		At 9am C.O. and representative officers visited No 2 Section Trenches. In evening took over No 2 Section of trenches.	
	7.V.15		Orders received that operations would commence tomorrow morning. All quiet in trenches during day. No. Pte Sharp sent to hospital with Cerebro spinal meningitis and died that night. Orders received at 6.45pm postponing operations for 24 hours. At 8.30pm enemy made a determined rush from rear and front on advanced sap held by Lt A.G. Grosz and 15 men. The attack was beaten off the enemy leaving 5 dead behind them. Our casualties have rifleman and 7 wounded including L/Sgt Moser [who showed great coolness and presence of mind and No 1027 Sgt Hocking T.J. who though badly wounded by opening report fire did much to check the enemy rush.] All quiet in trenches. [No 311. Sgt Harris S.J. killed between 3.30 – 4.30 H.Q. subjected to hail of trench Georgette. Conference of Coy Commanders then Co. decided knocks "CELLAR FARM" at 3am tomorrow. Lt A.G. Grosz sent into Hospital.	
	8.V.15			

1577 Wt.W10791/1773 500,000 1/15 D. D. & L. A.D.S.S./Forms/C. 2118.

WAR DIARY or INTELLIGENCE SUMMARY

Army Form C. 2118.

Place	Date	Hour	Summary of Events and Information	Remarks and references to Appendices
	9.5.15		At 4 a.m. the Battalion Staff established its Head Quarters at Redoubt S.E. in front of CELLAR FARM. The beginning of the engagement having been postponed until 5 a.m. the Battn. with the 2nd Rifle Brigade were withdrawn temporarily from the Brigade and placed in Divisional Reserve under G. Staff [2 M.x]. "B" & "C" Coys held the left half of No. 2 section of the trenches, "A" & "D" Coys being in support, the former at Redoubt 2 E., the latter at Redoubt 2 D. "A" Coy had been instructed from the trenches at midnight to leave that half of the section clear for the 25th Rifle Brigade machine gun section who only left "C" Coy and together with that Coy, had received orders to cover the left flank of the 13th London Regt. detailed to rush the Mine Crater at 5.40 a.m. Orders have been received that one left Coy had been employed & one "B" Coy & another "C" Coy 2nd hidden on digging a communication trench which should run along the line of the old sap and on the FROMELLES Regt. (the Last ??) of the German trench when captured. The digging began when the 25, & 50y the Bn had taken over our trenches. "B" & "D" Coy was detailed for this duty, (to take instructions regarding each time and place from the Coy Commander of the 29th X. The actual moves of the German trenches took place at 5.40 a.m. but the attack was afterwards held up.) At 9.3 a.m. "D" Coy was moved	

WAR DIARY or INTELLIGENCE SUMMARY

Army Form C.

Place	Date	Hour	Summary of Events and Information	Remarks and references to Appendices
LA CORDONNERIE	9.v.15		Forward from Redoubt 2D to the assembly trenches behind Allen farm previously occupied by 2 Scottish Rifles was trying the Coy into closer touch with H.Q. and withdrawing it from an area which was heavily shelled. At 10.20 a message was received from Capt Hayes to start work on communication trench as soon as possible. Orders were at once sent to Capt Enles ('B' Coy) to act accordingly. At 11.0 am Capt Enles reported in person that he had seen Capt Lofton (2nd 14th) and that they were both of opinion that it was not yet possible to start the work. At 11.42 am a message was despatched to Capt Hayes "Not yet possible to start work on communication trench will do so as soon as possible". At 1.30 pm the following received from Capt Enles was despatched to Capt Hayes "I have received orders from Brigadier commanding 23rd Bde that in event of our advance my Company will remain behind in trench Gareuin. The communication trench will not be built at present." At 3 pm the C.O. went in person to advance Brigade H.Q. in the trenches and received orders to reinforce with one platoon between 'B' and 'C' Coys. Lt Stacey's platoon was sent in the trenches and 2 Lt P. Chalken's platoon was sent to occupy Redoubt. During the afternoon the 1/3rd London Reserve handed over six prisoners of the 16 Hanover's Regiment who were	

WAR DIARY or INTELLIGENCE SUMMARY

Army Form C. 2118.

Place	Date	Hour	Summary of Events and Information	Remarks and references to Appendices
			despatched to the Rue du Bois cross roads. At 6.30pm C.O. again went forward H.Q. in the trenches and received orders to occupy the left half of No 2 section with the whole Battn. to enable further troops to withdraw. The C.O. endeavoured however to "A" and "D" Coys. known down to the trenches until 8.15pm. At 10.30pm a message was received from C.O. stating "You will remain in the trenches tonight. The sooner a strong party I have had orders to take charge of No 1+2 sections which the following day was sent. Have taken over 2R and 2S of trenches and a another must has taken over 2 Paros 2Q. My H.Q. went CELLAR FARM. telephone communication with Brigade throughout today. HQ. Total Casualties Rgmdr. Platoon remained intact. Capt. Frost, Subn. during the day 7 killed and 19 wounded (including Capt. Frost, Subn. and Tulley.)	
10.v.15			Desultory shelling throughout the day. Otherwise everything in the trenches normal. At 12.30pm received orders to proceed to today in right relieve induction 2.Q as the Reserve. Very heavy weather. Many known wounded brought in to the aid billet. Casualties during the day were 3 killed including Lt. Shaw, and	

Army Form C.

WAR DIARY
or
INTELLIGENCE SUMMARY.
(Erase heading not required.)

Instructions regarding War Diaries and Intelligence
Summaries are contained in F. S. Regs., Part II.
and the Staff Manual respectively. Title pages
will be prepared in manuscript.

Place	Date	Hour	Summary of Events and Information	Remarks and references to Appendices
LA GADONNERIE	10.V.15		5 wounded.	
do	11.	V.15	Heavy shelling on both sides from 12 noon to 1 p.m., 2-4 p.m. and 7-9. In the evening the Battalion was relieved by the 2 Seaforth Rifles and withdrew to billets along the Rue des QUESNES. "C" "D". Two companies went billeted "A" "B" at the Ellbow farms N.W. of PETILLON in support of No. 1 Sections. Companies in the Rue du QUESNES. trained parties for the second line posts Nos. 19, 20 & 21. Casualties during the day one killed and 8 wounded, including Capt. Moody.	
Hm do QUESNES	12.	V.15	Rest day. Casualties during the bivr. at LA GADONNERIE amounted to the action on the 9 & 10 together. Billeted are died in hospital of disease (Spotted fever) 2-41 wounded & 21 sent into hospital suffering chiefly from various breakdown. [Party sys whoim 1st Class? th supported 373 (Quehars...) both.	
do	13.	V.15	both of ... ... at ... ... 1/1 - 1/15	
do	14.	V.15	Nothing to Record. Capt. 3787 Pte Brewer, F.W. Smith	
do	15.	V.15.	Nothing to Record. No. 4474 Pte Pregnant L/Sgt was wounded.	

WAR DIARY or INTELLIGENCE SUMMARY.

Army Form C. 2118.

(Erase heading not required.)

Place	Date	Hour	Summary of Events and Information	Remarks and references to Appendices
Rue du QUESNES	16.v.15		Battn. took over No. 2 Section of trenches from 2 Scottish Rifles. No 3879 Pte Collins N.J. Killed.	
LA CORDONNERIE	17.v.15		All quiet in trenches. Two men wounded.	
do	18.v.15		All quiet in trenches. Four men wounded. Battn. relieved by 5 West Yorkshire Regt. at 8.30pm & moved into billets on Rue du BACQUEROT (WANGERIE) in support of E lines. Taking over second line posts 11.12.&13.	@Regt Party RueduPont Selby Tileries
WANGERIE to	19.v.15		Rest day. Took over in addition according to Post 14. 1st Maitland and 2nd Geoffry a July & 6 NCOi (sgt Vincent + sgt pearson, Pte Cari, Coon & Payne) were sent to the Highland Division at LE GOUVTURE to instruct in trench duties.	
do	20.v.15		Rest day.	
do	21.v.15		Took over E lines from 2 Mx. All quiet in trenches. 1st Maitland & 2nd L.I. ga. Kingdom C.Coy. were returned to their respective German trenches in front of FESTUBERT.	
FAUQUISSART	22.v.15		All quiet in trenches. No. 2163 Pte Collins, N.N. "A" Coy wounded.	
do	23.v.15		All quiet in trenches. During night trench mortar shell fell in trench wounding 6 men.	
do	24.v.15		General Davis C.B. Divisional Commander accompanied by General Pinney inspected the trenches.	
do	25.v.15		Enemy appeared to have lowered or altered the wire in front to the right our company and there seemed no altered appearance of their parapet as a precautionary	

WAR DIARY
or
INTELLIGENCE SUMMARY.
(Erase heading not required.)

Army Form C. 2118.

Place	Date	Hour	Summary of Events and Information	Remarks and references to Appendices
			reserve to trench line was reinforced by the four platoons holding the supporting posts being replaced in those posts by a supporting company of the 2nd Middlesex. Two machine guns were brought up from the 2nd Middlesex making places in the trenches & the other in Redoubt E1. The Grenadier platoon was also brought up.	
FAUQUISSART	26.V.15		German wire in front of right Company seen to be replaced. Normal conditions therefore resumed. All quiet in trenches. Two men wounded. During early hours of morning a patrol from "C" Company visited the ruined house on Rue D'ENFER 200 yards in front of our lines. Five minutes after they left the house blew up.	
do	27.V.15		Relieved in trenches by 2 Middx at 8.45pm and billets at WANGERIE in Brigade reserve. "B" Coy was kept in state of constant readiness as supporting Coy whilst "C" Coy occupied 2nd Liverpools. 1 platoon at No.11, 2 platoons at No.12, 2 sections at No.13 and 2 sections at No.74.	
ANGERIE	28.V.15		Regt Nothing to record except desultory shelling.	
do	29.V.15		Nothing to record except desultory shelling.	

Army Form C. 2118.

WAR DIARY
or
INTELLIGENCE SUMMARY.

(Erase heading not required.)

Instructions regarding War Diaries and Intelligence Summaries are contained in F. S. Regs., Part II. and the Staff Manual respectively. Title pages will be prepared in manuscript.

Place	Date	Hour	Summary of Events and Information	Remarks and references to Appendices
WANGERIE	30.V.15		Capt. & Adj. Bowen left for England for seven days leave. The temporary vacancy being filled by Lieut J.K. Maitland.	
do.	31.V.15		On the reorganisation of the second line front the Batt. took over no 10 Post from the Rifle Brigade and handed over no. 14 Post to the 2nd Scot. Rifles. VIII 9th Division taken over as part of the 4th Corps and future Indian Corps.	

G.V.F____
Lieut. Col. Commdg.
1st BATT. 7th MIDDLESEX REGT.

____
Capt. & Adjt.
1st BATT. 7th MIDDLESEX REGT.

23rd Inf. Bde.
8th Division

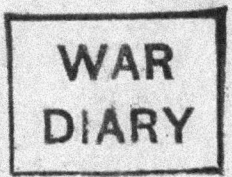

1/7th Battalion

THE MIDDLESEX REGIMENT

APRIL 1915

121/5318

8th Division.

7th Middlesex.

Vol II 1 — 30.4.15.

Army Form C. 2118.

WAR DIARY
or
INTELLIGENCE SUMMARY.
(Erase heading not required.)

Instructions regarding War Diaries and Intelligence Summaries are contained in F.S. Regs., Part II. and the Staff Manual respectively. Title pages will be prepared in manuscript.

Hour, Date, Place	Summary of Events and Information	Remarks and references to Appendices
FLEURBAIX 1.iv.15	Rest day	
2.iv.15	Bly changes its billets for farmhouses in the Rue du VIF to	
3.iv.15	"C" Coy. moves from RUE du PIERRE to FROG FARM in support of section 5 of the Tenth line. Major S. King went into hospital this day.	
4.iv.15	Disturbed orders were received concerning the second line posts in the neighbourhood of FLEUR B.H. (namely 23, 24, 25, & 27, 28 & 29. 2/4th R.H.E. being tooth up. 2nd/4th attached to an A.D.C. to the hospital. Between 2.30 and 3.30 about 1/2 Shells fell in the area apparently from the Howitzer Battery type of FROMELLES German slightly wounded. The various type of	
5.iv.15	Hand Grenades were shown to their the day. Others were received t.y. into Durament Reserved. During the morning the Church was again shelled by a Howitzer Battery presumed coming from FROMELLES between 11 & 11.30 am two men being wounded No 2379 Pte Hearn A Coy & No 3789 Pte Hocking D Coy). Shelling was again resumed between 11h.30 pm & at 4.h.30 Pm.	
6.iv.15	Fresh offr (Lieut "C" Coy) moved into Divisional Reserve at BAC ST MAUR. Pte etc...	Signed onr

(73989) W4141-463. 400,000. 9/14. H&J.Ltd. Forms/C. 2118/10.

Army Form C. 2118.

WAR DIARY
or
INTELLIGENCE SUMMARY.
(Erase heading not required.)

Instructions regarding War Diaries and Intelligence Summaries are contained in F.S. Regs., Part II. and the Staff Manual respectively. Title pages will be prepared in manuscript.

Hour, Date, Place	Summary of Events and Information	Remarks and references to Appendices
BAC ST MAUR 7.iv.15.	Lancashire Regt. The remaining Coy from Doval Reserve arrived at 9.30pm.	
8.iv.15.	Route marching by companies. Lieut H Kingsgrove from Hosp.	
	Orders were received to take over No 1 sector of trenches for 6 days on April 12th.	
9.iv.15	Route marching by companies	
10.iv.15	Nothing to Report. Operation orders for move on 12th issued.	
11.iv.15	At 9.15 am Co. and representatives visited No 1. Section of trench line. Relief by 1/R hits.	
12.iv.15	At 6.45pm Battn. marched to LE TROU and took over No 1. Section of trenches. Trenches held by Companies are shown in attached sheet. No additional fire at M hole in the T. knee stream Redoubt – Montauban, Pickem Redoubte 7R. & C. L things (& K) and Lt. Ship line of trenches before Montauban were in reserve	Carithers

Army Form C. 2118.

WAR DIARY
or
INTELLIGENCE SUMMARY.
(Erase heading not required.)

Hour, Date, Place	Summary of Events and Information	Remarks and references to Appendices
LE TROU 13.iv.15	Considerable work done on enemy's wire during the night. Otherwise nothing of interest. During the morning General Anderson and the Brigade Major visited the trenches. About 6.30 pm Lt. Col. Sir Henry Rawlinson and Staff arrived & made their inspection. Two casualties during the day. No. 1749 Pte Davis killed & No. 2414 Pte Lawrie T.W. "C" Coy wounded.	
14.iv.15	All quiet in the trenches. One casualty [No 2415 Pte Strange "A" Coy.]	
15.iv.15	During the night activity of our Scouts prevented enemy patrols leaving the trenches. [During the morning General PINNEY inspected the trenches. No. 3836 Pte Savage Wright R.A.C. Coy wounded.	
16.iv.15	During night enemy did considerable work on barbed wire and sent out a considerable party of workmakers. One casualty [No. 1767 Pte Morley J.N. "A" Coy Killed]	

Army Form C. 2118.

WAR DIARY
or
INTELLIGENCE SUMMARY.
(Erase heading not required.)

Instructions regarding War Diaries and Intelligence Summaries are contained in F.S. Regs., Part II. and the Staff Manual respectively. Title pages will be prepared in manuscript.

Place	Date	Hour	Summary of Events and Information	Remarks and references to Appendices
LE TROU	17.IV.15		All quiet in trenches. No 1960 Pte Small, M was wounded.	
	18.IV.15		During the night a German working party was thought to have approached from our right. machine gun fire. In the evening the Battn. was relieved by the 2nd. Middx Regt. & took over their Billets. HQ & "B" & "A" Coy Rue du QUESNES. "C" & "D" at farm in Square N.1.a.	
Rue du QUESNES	19.IV.15		The Grenadiers returned to duty (see Gittens & Snape & Brig. Analysis). Section of trenchline left at PETILLON in support of No 1 Section of trenchline. Reat. day. Conference at Brigade HQ at 2 p.m. 2/Lt Donlaing returned to duty from to Brigade Staff.	
	20.IV.15		All Officers reconnoitred assembly trenches at LE TROU. The C.O., G.A.H. Bower and No 955 L/Cpl W.H. Willis, the latter for gallant conduct in the trenches where both at LA BOUTILLERIE and LE TROU he was out aiding night after night close up to the enemys lines setting a very valuable example to his Comrades.	
"	Cont. 21. 20.iv.15		2/Lt R.B. Scott reported for duty this day & was posted to "D" Coy. A field general Courtmartial was held this day on No 227 L/Cpl Mendes, J.S. "D" Coy found asleep whilst sentry in the trenches. He was found guilty & sentenced to 3 months field punishment No 1.	

Army Form C. 2118.

WAR DIARY
or
INTELLIGENCE SUMMARY.

(Erase heading not required.)

Place	Date	Hour	Summary of Events and Information	Remarks and references to Appendices
RUE du QUESNES	22.IV.15		C.O. attended a Brigade Conference at No. 2 Section Brigade lines at 10 a.m. In the afternoon possible future operations explained to all officers. Lt Stacey despatched to ROUEN to fetch up draft.	
"	23.IV.15		Orders received to go into Divisional Reserve tomorrow and to take over billets of 4th K.O.Y.L.I. in neighbourhood of LE CRUSEOBEAU	
"	24.IV.15		The Battn went into Divisional Reserve in neighbourhood of LE CRUSEOBEAU marching off at 9 p.m. "A" coy did not move until 7.45 p.m.	
LE CRUSEOBEAU	25.IV.15		Rest day. Lieut C.N. Stacey returned from ROUEN with a draft of [Sgd 43 ??] men of whom 4 were accidentally left behind at HAZEBROUCK.	
"	26.IV.15		"A" & "D" Coys executed a tactical route march. "B" & "C" Coys practised attack formations.	
"	27.IV.15		The Battalion was exercised in moving across country under shell fire the Brigadier being present.	
"	28.IV.15		"B" & "C" Coys executed a tactical route march. "A" & "D" Coys practised attack formations.	
"	29.IV.15		"A" & "D" Coys executed a tactical route march. "B" & "C" Coys practised attack formations.	
"	30.IV.15		Night working parties were furnished as follows for work under R.E. 157 men under Capt Wincely worked at CROIX BLANCHE reports at 8.0 p.m. for work under 15th Field Coy R.E.	

Capt R ???
1577 Wt W10791/1773 500,000 1/15 D.D.&L. A.D.S.S./Forms/C. 2118.

Army Form C. 2118.

WAR DIARY
or
INTELLIGENCE SUMMARY.
(Erase heading not required.)

Place	Date	Hour	Summary of Events and Information	Remarks and references to Appendices
LE CROSEOBEAU	30.IV.15		At PETILLON at 8.0pm 100 men under Capt Tully for work under 2nd Field Coy R.E. At PETILLON at 8.30pm 150 men under Capt Foot tat 9.30pm 100 men under Capt Eales for work under 1oist Home Counties Field Coy R.E.	

Scott Power
Capt Adjt
1/7 Middlesex Regt

[signature]
Lieut. Col. Commdg.
1st BATT. 7th MIDDLESEX REGT.

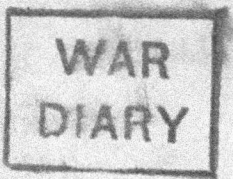

23rd Inf. Bde.
8th Divn.

Bn. disembarked Harve from U.K. 13. 3. 15.

Bn. joined 23rd Inf. Bde. 15. 3. 15.

1/7th Battalion

THE MIDDLESEX REGIMENT

14th FEBRUARY to 31st MARCH 1 9 1 5.

Disembarked
Home from
England 13.3.15.

Joined 23 Bn 15.3.15

23rd Brigade
8
117 Middlesex
Vol I 14.2 — 31.3.15

Army Form C. 2118.

WAR DIARY
INTELLIGENCE SUMMARY.
(Erase heading not required.)

Hour, Date, Place	Summary of Events and Information	Remarks and references to Appendices
	CONFIDENTIAL. War Diary of 1/7th Middlesex Regt from 14th February 1915 to 31st March 1915.	

Instructions regarding War Diaries and Intelligence Summaries are contained in F.S. Regs., Part II and the Staff Manual respectively. Title pages will be prepared in manuscript.

1/7th BN. THE MIDDLESEX REGIMENT.

1915.

February.   AVONMOUTH.   Appendix.

14th.   4 a.m.   Landed at Avonmouth from Gibraltar and proceeded to High Barnet to mobilize.

March.

HIGH BARNET.

9th.   6 p.m.   Reported mobilization completed and ready to move.

10th.   12 noon. Received order "hold yourself in readiness to move Friday".
         10 p.m.   Received Embarkation order for Friday 12th.

12th.   Proceeded to New Barnet to entrain for Southampton trains left New Barnet at 7.30 a.m, 9.10 a.m. & 10.50 a.m. Embarked on S.S. MUNICH and left Southampton 9.30 pm. proceeding without escort. Strength 26 Officers and 811 Other Ranks. Transport with 4 Officers and 96 Other Ranks on the Inventa. Latter ship travelled under escort.

HAVRE.

13th.   6.15 a.m. Disembarked and marched to No.2 Rest Camp at BLEVILLE (BLEVILLE). Transport and detachment from Inventa joining later in the day. Completed deficiencies of equipment. The Interpreter Deconies of the 45th Territorial Infantry reported for duty. Received orders to entrain tomorrow less 2 platoons.

14th.   1 p.m.   Battalion entrained at Havre at 1 p.m. leaving Station at 4.30 p.m. Two platoons (Nos.3 & 4) left at rest Camp consisting of 85 N.C.O's & men under Lt. Groser and 2.Lt. P. Challen also left behind Orderly Room Sergeant (H.K. King), 4 sick men and 3 drummers under age entraining strength therefore 28 Officers &   men.

1915.

| March. | | LA GORGUE. | Appendix. |

15th. 1.30 p.m. Arrived at LA GORGUE and moved into billets, A.Coy. (less 2 platoons), "C" Coy. & M.G. section at School, "D" Coy. and transport at Farm. "B" Coy. Rue de Gendarmerie, H.Q. in House next to Post Office. Attached 23rd Brigade VIII Division 4th Corps.

16th. Returned Goatskin coats to Ordnance.

17th. 6 a.m. Received orders to move at 11 a.m. and go into fresh Billets in neighbourhood of LA FLINQUE, H.Q. and C & D Companies on road E of LA FLINQUE, A & B on Road S.W. of LA FLINQUE. The Battalion was met by its Brigade Commander General PINNEY after passing LE DRUMEZ and defiled past the Divisional Commander General DAVIES. The Transport was parked on road 1½ miles W. of LA FLINQUE. General Pinney visited the troops in their billets in the afternoon.

LA FLINQUE.

18th. Exchanged 2 N.C.O's & 6 privates per platoon with 2/Mx & a Machine Gun Corporal for instructional purposes, the exchange to last for one week. Men were occupied during the day in improving existing dugouts and constructing new ones. During the afternoon the Transport lines were subjected to shell fire, 38 shells bursting in the lines but no damage to man or beast. Transport was moved back to le DRUMEZ. At 6.30 p.m. 2 platoons under 2.Lt. A.R. Williamson reported at cross roads S.E. of B in BACQUEROT for work under 15th Field Company, R.E. "B" Coy. reported at same hour at R in Rue on RUE du BACQUEROY for work under

Map Sheet 36

19th. 1st Home Counties Field Coy R.E. C.O. and Adjutant attended a Conference at H.Q. "C" lines at 9 a.m. Each company was ordered to attack one platoon to a corresponding company of the

1:40,000. LILLE. Revised system of squaring.

1915.

March.

19th.
(Ctd).

2nd Middlesex for 48 hours duty in the trenches to report at 2 Middx H.Q. at 6.30 p.m. Platoons detailed Lt. Staceys A.Coy, Lt. Shiplins B.Coy, 2.Lt. F.Smith's C.Coy. & Lt. Hurds D.Coy. Capt. Cossar with 2.Lt.Ashby's & 2.Lt. Chennells platoons were ordered to report at same place and time as reinforcement to the reserve of "C" lines. Each man was equipped with 2 empty sandbags. 2 days rations & 100 rounds extra ammunition. In addition one Officer per Coy. viz: Maj. S. King, "C" Coy. Capt.Frost, "D" Coy, Capt. Moody, "A" Coy. & Capt. Gillett "B" Coy. were attached to corresponding Coys. 2 Middlesex for 48 hours duty in the trenches for instructional purposes, reporting at 4 p.m. Two working parties of 100 men under Capt. Smith and 150 men under Capt. Tully were ordered to report at 6.30 p.m. at Road Junction M,22,b,8,8 for work under 15 Field Coy. R.E. and at M.22 central on RUE du BACQUEROT for work under 1st Home Counties Field Company, R.E. respectively. The 2 platoons left at HAVRE, joined the Bn. at 9 pm.

Appendix.

Geographical series Gen. Staff No. 2743.

20th.

The Commanding Officer spent the day in C lines section 4 having spent the night at C lines Head Quarters. The following casualties occurred in the trenches in No.15 Platoon from rifle fire Killed at 6.45 a.m. No. 1664 Pte. Phillips, J.E. slightly wounded at 8.30 a.m. No.2295 Pte. Carter A.J. Private Phillips was buried in the trenches.
About 3 p.m. Head Quarters "C" lines was shelled and burnt to the ground. In the fire the rifles and kits of half the men of the 2 platoons in reserve were destroyed. All the possessions of Capt. Cossar & 2.Lt. Chennell were also destroyed.
A German aeroplane passed over H.Q. going W. about 8.30 a.m. & returned about 9 a.m. A few shells

1915.

March.   Appendix.

20th.   fell in the neighbourhood of
(Ctd).   H.Q. about 4 p.m.
            Working parties of 100 men
            under Capt. Smith & 150 men
            under Capt. Tully reported at
            xxxxxxxxxx the former at 7 pm.
            and the latter at 6.30 pm. the
            respective rendezvous being
            Road Junc. Sq. M.22.b.8.8. &
            M.22 central to work under 15th
            Field Coy. R.E. & 1st Home
            Counties R.E.

21st.   At 2 pm. the Battalion marched
            back to LA GORGUE and took over
            fresh billets. The 4 platoons
            from the trenches and the 2
            reserve platoons attached to
            the 2nd Middx. did not arrive
            until after midnight. The
            former had sustained one casualty
            in Lt. Hurd's platoon No.
            Pte. Sweetsur. The 2 platoons
            in reserve had been heavily
            shelled in the afternoon but had
            sustained no casualties.

            LA GORGUE.

22nd.   Kept as a rest day. Orders were
            received to move to SAILLY
            tomorrow in order to take over
            trenches held by Canadian
            Division on the 25th.

23rd.   About midday a waggon load of
            hand grenades blew up in "C" Coys.
            billeting areas seriously injuring
            Cpl. Knowers P. and an N.C.O.
            attached from the 2nd Battn. at
            2 p.m. the Battn. moved off to
            take over fresh billets at
            BAC ST. MAUR.

            BAC ST. MAUR.

24th.   At 9.30 a.m. a conference was
            held at Bde.H.Q. to explain
            arrangements for taking over
            section 4 of the trench line
            now held by the 8th Canadian
            Regt.   During the afternoon
            the Battn. Staff and representative
            Officers visited the trenches
            personally to acquaint themselves
            with the arrangements there.

1915.

March.   Appendix.

25th.   At 5.30 p.m. the Battn.
                marched via FLEURBAIX and
                CROIX MARECHAL to take over
                section 4 of the trench line
                at LA BOUTILLERIE. At 8.30 pm.
                the relief of the 8th Canadian
                Rgt. had been effected. "C"
                Coy. held portion of trenches
                on our right of main road, "D"
                Coy. with Machine Gun section
                the remainder. "A" Coy. was
                in support "B" Coy. in reserve
                both billeted along the road.
                Head Quarters at large farm at
                LA BOUTILLERIE. The transport
                which moved at 4 pm. was parked
                along the Rue de 1 PIERRE. The
                Grenadier Platoon (1 N.C.O. &
                5 men per Company) was formed
                this day under 2.Lt. Chennell
                and marched & remained with
                the Transport. Lieut. H.K.King
                went into Hospital this day.

                LA BOUTILLERIE.

26th.   The Major commanding supporting
                Battery called at 10.30 a.m.
                At 11 a.m. the Brigade Major
                and Adjutant 6th Scottish
                Rifles called to discuss
                arrangements for instruction of
                that Battn. in trench duties.
                At ~~4.30 pm~~. 3.30 pm Major
                Commanding 15th Field Company R.E.
                visited the trenches. At 4 pm
                representatives of 6th Scottish
                Rifles visited the trenches.
                The same Battn. handed over 4
                periscopes. In the trenches
                no unusual occurrence took
                place during the 24 hours. During
                the day one man No. 1422 Pte. Watt,
                G. was severely wounded.

27th.   Nothing to report from trenches
                No.~~2111~~ 3875 Pte. Thompson W.F.
                D.Coy. accidentally wounded.
                At 10 am. C.O. took O.C. and
                Adjt. 6th Scottish Rifles round
                the trenches and defended
                localities. Col. Hayes and
                Brigade Major also visited trenches.
                During afternoon between 4 & 5 pm
                the area was shelled by enemy's
                howitzers for one hour. About
                30 shells fell at first in
                neighbourhood of H.Q. afterwards
                in front of nearest billets.
                No damage was done. During the
                evening 4 platoons 6th Scottish
                Rifles entered the trenches for the

1915.

March.   Appendix.

27th.   night. Pte. Watts died of
(Ctd).   his wounds this day.

28th.   Nothing to report from trenches.
                One casualty No. 3817 Pte.
                Markwick who was killed. During
                the evening "A" Coy. relieved "C"
                Coy, in right section & "B"
                relieved "D" in left section. Four
                platoons from 6th Scottish Rifles
                again visited the trenches.
                Report received that Cpl. Knowers
                died on his way to Hospital on
                23rd & was buried at MERVILLE.

29th.   Nothing to Report. No casualties.
                Four platoons 6th Scottish Rifles
                spent night in trenches.

30th.   Nothing to Report. One man
                slightly wounded. Lce.Cpl.
                Pendleton "B" Coy, Pte.Kittle,
                "D" Coy. accidentally shot himself
                in foot. Four platoons 6th Scottish
                Rifles went into trenches for the
                night. Orders received to take
                over Billets of 6th Scottish
                Rifles tomorrow who will replace
                us in the trenches.

31st.   At 8 a.m. the General inspected
                the trenches. 2.Lt. Ronald M.E.
                King was nominated as an assistant
                A.D.C. In the evening the Battalion
                was relieved by the 6th Scottish
                Rifles and moved into the Billets
                of that Battn.H.Q. and A & D.Coys.
                in FLEURBAIX. B & C Coys. on
                RUE DEL PIERRE.

                                G.A.H. BOWER, Capt. & Adj.
                                1/7 Middlesex Regt.

1/7th BN. THE MIDDLESEX REGIMENT.

1915.

| February. | | AVONMOUTH. | Appendix. |

14th. 4 a.m. Landed at Avonmouth xx from Gibraltar and proceeded to High Barnet to mobilize.

March.

HIGH BARNET.

9th. 6 p.m. Reported mobilization completed and ready to move.

10th. 12 noon. Received order "hold yourself in readiness to move Friday".
10 p.m. Received Embarkation order for Friday 12th.

12th. Proceeded to New Barnet to entrain for Southampton trains left New Barnet at 7.30 a.m, 9.10 a.m. & 10.50 a.m. Embarked on S.S. MUNICH and left Southampton 9.30 pm. proceeding without escort. Strength 26 Officers and 811 Other Ranks. Transport with 4 Officers and 96 Other Ranks on the Inventa. Latter ship travelled under escort.

HAVRE.

13th. 6.15 a.m. Disembarked and marched to No.2 Rest Camp at BLEVILLE (BLEVILLE). Transport and detachment from Inventa joining later in the day. Completed deficiencies of equipment. The Interpreter Deconies of the 45th Territorial Infantry reported for duty. Received orders to entrain tomorrow less 2 platoons.

14th. 1 p.m. Battalion entrained at Havre at 1 p.m. leaving Station at 4.30 p.m. Two platoons (Nos.3 & 4) left at rest Camp consisting of 85 N.C.O's & men under Lt. Groser and 2.Lt. P. Challen also left behind Orderly Room Sergeant (H.K. King), 4 sick men and 3 drummers under age entraining strength therefore 28 Officers &   men.

1915.

March. **LA GORGUE.** Appendix.

15th. 1.30 p.m. Arrived at LA GORGUE and moved into billets, A.Coy. (less 2 platoons), "C" Coy. & M.G. section at School, "D" Coy. and transport at Farm. "B" Coy. Rue de Gendarmerie, H.Q. in House next to Post Office. Attached 23rd Brigade VIII Division 4th Corps.

16th. Returned Goatskin coats to Ordnance.

17th. 6 a.m. Received orders to move at 11 a.m. and go into fresh Billets in neighbourhood of LA FLINQUE, H.Q. and C & D Companies on road E of LA FLINQUE, A & B on Road S.W. of LA FLINQUE. The Battalion was met by its Brigade Commander General PINNEY after passing LE DRUMEZ and defiled past the Divisional Commander General DAVIES. The Transport was parked on road 1½ miles W. of LA FLINQUE. General Pinney visited the troops in their billets in the afternoon.

LA FLINQUE.

18th. Exchanged 2 N.C.O's & 6 privates per platoon with 2/Mx & a Machine Gun Corporal for instructional purposes, the exchange to last for one week. Men were occupied during the day in improving existing dugouts and constructing new ones. During the afternoon the Transport lines were subjected to shell fire, 38 shells bursting in the lines but no damage to man or beast. Transport was moved back to le DRUMEZ. At 6.30 p.m. 2 platoons under 2.Lt. A.R. Williamson reported at cross roads S.E. of B in BACQUEROT for work under 15th Field Company, R.E. "B" Coy. reported at same hour at R in Rue RUE du BACQUEROY for work under

19th. 1st Home Counties Field Coy R.E. C.O. and Adjutant attended a Conference at H.Q. "O" lines at 9 a.m. Each company was ordered to attack one platoon to a corresponding company of the

Map Sheet 36 1:40,000. LILLE. Revised system of squaring.

1915.

March.

19th.
(Ctd).

2nd Middlesex for 48 hours duty in the trenches to report at 2 Middx H.Q. at 6.30 p.m. Platoons detailed Lt. Staceys A.Coy, Lt. Shiplins B.Coy, 2.Lt. F.Smith's C.Coy. & Lt. Hurds D.Coy. Capt. Cossar with 2.Lt.Ashby's & 2.Lt. Chennells platoons were ordered to report at same place and time as reinforcement to the reserve of "C" lines. Each man was equipped with 2 empty sandbags. 2 days rations & 100 rounds extra ammunition. In addition one Officer per Coy. viz: Maj. S. King, "C" Coy. Capt.Frost, "D" Coy, Capt. Moody, "A" Coy. & Capt. Gillett "B" Coy. were attached to corresponding Coys. 2 Middlesex for 48 hours duty in the trenches for instructional purposes, reporting at 4 p.m. Two working parties of 100 men under Capt. Smith and 150 men under Capt. Tully were ordered to report at 6.30 p.m. at Road Junction M.22,b,8,8 for work under 15 Field Coy. R.E. and at M.22 central on RUE du BACQUEROT for work under 1st Home Counties Field Company, R.E. respectively. The 2 platoons left at HAVRE, joined the Bn. at 9 pm.

Appendix.

Geographical series Gen. Staff No. 2743.

20th.

The Commanding Officer spent the day in C lines section 4 having spent the night at C lines Head Quarters. The following casualties occurred in the trenches in No.15 Platoon from rifle fire Killed at 6.45 a.m. No. 1664 Pte. Phillips, J.E. slightly wounded at 8.30 a.m. No.2295 Pte. Carter A.J. Private Phillips was buried in the trenches.
About 3 p.m. Head Quarters "C" lines was shelled and burnt to the ground. In the fire the rifles and kits of half the men of the 2 platoons in reserve were destroyed. All the possessions of Capt. Cossar & 2.Lt. Chennell were also destroyed.
A German aeroplane passed over H.Q. going W. about 8.30 a.m. & returned about 9 a.m. A few shells

1915.

March.   Appendix.

20th.   fell in the neighbourhood of
(Ctd).   H.Q. about 4 p.m.
                Working parties of 100 men
                under Capt. Smith & 150 men
                under Capt. Tully reported
                the former at 7 pm.
                and the latter at 6.30 pm. the
                respective rendezvous being
                Road Junc. Sq. M.22.b.8.8. &
                M.22 central to work under 15th
                Field Coy. R.E. & 1st Home
                Counties R.E.

21st.   At 2 pm. the Battalion marched
                back to LA GORGUE and took over
                fresh billets. The 4 platoons
                from the trenches and the 2
                reserve platoons attached to
                the 2nd Middx. did not arrive
                until after midnight. The
                former had sustained one casualty
                in Lt. Hurd's platoon No.
                Pte. Sweetsur. The 2 platoons
                in reserve had been heavily
                shelled in the afternoon but had
                sustained no casualties.

                LA GORGUE.

22nd.   Kept as a rest day. Orders were
                received to move to SAILLY
                tomorrow in order to take over
                trenches held by Canadian
                Division on the 25th.

23rd.   About midday a waggon load of
                hand grenades blew up in "C" Coys.
                billeting areas seriously injuring
                Cpl. Knowers P. and an N.C.O.
                attached from the 2nd Battn. at
                2 p.m. the Battn. moved off to
                take over fresh billets at
                BAC ST. MAUR.

                BAC ST. MAUR.

24th.   At 9.30 a.m. a conference was
                held at Bde.H.Q. to explain
                arrangements for taking over
                section 4 of the trench line
                now held by the 8th Canadian
                Regt.   During the afternoon
                the Battn. Staff and representative
                Officers visited the trenches
                personally to acquaint themselves
                with the arrangements there.

1915.

March.   Appendix.

25th.   At 5.30 p.m. the Battn.
marched via FLEURBAIX and
CROIX MARECHAL to take over
section 4 of the trench line
at LA BOUTILLERIE. At 8.30 pm.
the relief of the 8th Canadian
Rgt. had been effected. "C"
Coy. held portion of trenches
on our right of main road, "D"
Coy. with Machine Gun section
the remainder. "A" Coy. was
in support "B" Coy. in reserve
both billeted along the road.
Head Quarters at large farm at
LA BOUTILLERIE. The transport
which moved at 4 pm. was parked
along the Rue de l PIERRE. The
Grenadier Platoon (1 N.C.O. &
5 men per Company) was formed
this day under 2.Lt. Chennell
and marched & remained with
the Transport. Lieut. H.K.King
went into Hospital this day.

LA BOUTILLERIE.

26th.   The Major commanding supporting
Battery called at 10.30 a.m.
At 11 a.m. the Brigade Major
and Adjutant 6th Scottish
Rifles called to discuss
arrangements for instruction of
that Battn. in trench duties.
At 3.30 pm Major
Commanding 15th Field Company R.E.
visited the trenches. At 4 pm
representatives of 6th Scottish
Rifles visited the trenches.
The same Battn. handed over 4
periscopes. In the trenches
no unusual occurrence took
place during the 24 hours. During
the day one man No. 1422 Pte. Watt,
G. was severely wounded.

27th.   Nothing to report from trenches
No. 3875 Pte. Thompson W.F.
D.Coy. accidentally wounded.
At 10 am. C.O. took O.C. and
Adjt. 6th Scottish Rifles round
the trenches and defended
localities. Col. Hayes and
Brigade Major also visited trenches.
During afternoon between 4 & 5 pm
the area was shelled by enemy's
howitzers for one hour. About
30 shells fell at first in
neighbourhood of H.Q. afterwards
in front of nearest billets.
No damage was done. During the
evening 4 platoons 6th Scottish
Rifles entered the trenches for the

1915.

March.   Appendix.

27th.   night. Pte. Watts died of
(Ctd).   his wounds this day.

28th.   Nothing to report from trenches.
                 One casualty No. 3817 Pte.
                 Markwick who was killed. During
                 the evening "A" Coy. relieved "C"
                 Coy, in right section & "B"
                 relieved "D" in left section. Four
                 platoons from 6th Scottish Rifles
                 again visited the trenches.
                 Report received that Cpl. Knowers
                 died on his way to Hospital on
                 23rd & was buried at MERVILLE.

29th.   Nothing to Report. No casualties.
                 Four platoons 6th Scottish Rifles
                 spent night in trenches.

30th.   Nothing to Report. One man
                 slightly wounded. Lce.Cpl.
                 Pendleton "B" Coy, Pte.Kittle,
                 "D" Coy. accidentally shot himself
                 in foot. Four platoons 6th Scottish
                 Rifles went into trenches for the
                 night. Orders received to take
                 over Billets of 6th Scottish
                 Rifles tomorrow who will replace
                 us in the trenches.

31st.   At 8 a.m. the General inspected
                 the trenches. 2.Lt. Ronald M.E.
                 King was nominated as an assistant
                 A.D.C. In the evening the Battalion
                 was relieved by the 6th Scottish
                 Rifles and moved into the Billets
                 of that Battn.H.Q. and A & D.Coys.
                 in FLEURBAIX. B & C Coys. on
                 RUE DEL PIERRE.

                               G.A.H. BOWER, Capt. & Adj.
                               1/7 Middlesex Regt.

1/7th BN. THE MIDDLESEX REGIMENT.

1915.

February.		AVONMOUTH.	Appendix.
14th.	4 a.m.	Landed at Avonmouth from Gibraltar and proceeded to High Barnet to mobilise.	
March.			
		HIGH BARNET.	
9th.	6 p.m.	Reported mobilization completed and ready to move.	
10th.	12 noon.	Received order "hold yourself in readiness to move Friday".	
	10 p.m.	Received Embarkation order for Friday 12th.	
12th.		Proceeded to New Barnet to entrain for Southampton trains left New Barnet at 7.30 a.m, 9.10 a.m. & 10.50 a.m. Embarked on S.S. MUNICH and left Southampton 9.30 pm. proceeding without escort. Strength 26 Officers and 811 Other Ranks. Transport with 4 Officers and 96 Other Ranks on the Inventa. Latter ship travelled under escort.	
		HAVRE.	
13th.	6.15 a.m.	Disembarked and marched to No.2 Rest Camp at BLEVILLE (BLEVILLE). Transport and detachment from Inventa joining later in the day. Completed deficiencies of equipment. The Interpreter Deconies of the 45th Territorial Infantry reported for duty. Received orders to entrain tomorrow less 2 platoons.	
14th.	1 p.m.	Battalion entrained at Havre at 1 p.m. leaving Station at 4.30 p.m. Two platoons (Nos.3 & 4) left at rest Camp consisting of 85 N.C.O's & men under Lt. Groser and 2.Lt. F. Challen also left behind Orderly Room Sergeant (R.X. King), 4 sick men and 3 drummers under age entraining strength therefore 26 Officers & men.	

1915.

March.   LA GORGUE.   Appendix.

15th. 1.30   Arrived at LA GORGUE and
      p.m.   moved into billets, A.Coy.
             (less 2 platoons), "C" Coy. &
             M.G. section at School, "D" Coy.
             and transport at Farm. "B" Coy.
             Rue de Gendarmerie, H.Q. in
             House next to Post Office.
             Attached 23rd Brigade VIII
             Division 4th Corps.

16th.   Returned Goatskin coats to
             Ordnance.

17th. 6 a.m. Received orders to move at
             11 a.m. and go into fresh
             Billets in neighbourhood of
             LA FLINQUE. H.Q. and C & D
             Companies on road E of LA
             FLINQUE, A & B on Road S.W. of
             LA FLINQUE. The Battalion was
             met by its Brigade Commander
             General PINNEY after passing LE
             DRUMEZ and defiled past the
             Divisional Commander General
             DAVIES. The Transport was
             parked on road 1½ miles W. of
             LA FLINQUE. General Pinney
             visited the troops in their
             billets in the afternoon.

          LA FLINQUE.

18th.   Exchanged 2 N.C.O's & 6 privates
             per platoon with 2/Mx & a Machine
             Gun Corporal for instructional
             purposes, the exchange to last
             for one week.   Men were
             occupied during the day in
             improving existing dugouts and
             constructing new ones.   During
             the afternoon the Transport lines
             were subjected to shell fire, 38
             shells bursting in the lines but
             no damage to man or beast.
             Transport was moved back to le
             DRUMEZ.   At 6.30 p.m. 2
             platoons under 2.Lt. A.R. Williamson
             reported at cross roads S.E. of B
             in BACQUEROT for work under 15th
             Field Company, R.E.   "B" Coy.
             reported at same hour at H in Rue   Map Sheet
             RUE du BACQUEROT for work under   36
19th,   1st Home Counties Field Coy R.E.   1:40,000.
             C.O. and Adjutant attended a   LILLE.
             Conference at H.Q. "C" lines
             at 9 a.m.   Each company was   Revised
             ordered to attack one platoon   system of
             to a corresponding company of the   squaring.

1915.

March.

19th.
(Ctd).

2nd Middlesex for 48 hours duty in the trenches to report at 2 Middx H.Q. at 6.30 p.m. Platoons detailed Lt. Stacey's A.Coy, Lt. Shipline B.Coy, 2.Lt. F.Smith's C.Coy, & Lt. Burds D.Coy. Capt. Cossar with 2.Lt.Ashby's & 2.Lt. Chennells platoons were ordered to report at same place and time as reinforcement to the reserve of "C" lines. Each man was equipped with 2 empty sandbags. 2 days rations & 100 rounds extra ammunition. In addition one Officer per Coy. viz: Maj. S. King, "C" Coy. Capt.Frost, "D" Coy, Capt. Moody, "A" Coy. & Capt. Gillett "B" Coy. were attached to corresponding Coys. 2 Middlesex for 48 hours duty in the trenches for instructional purposes, reporting at 4 p.m. Two working parties of 100 men under Capt. Smith and 150 men under Capt. Tully were ordered to report at 6.30 p.m. at Road Junction M.22.b.6.8 for work under 15 Field Coy. R.E. and at M.22 central on RUE du BACQUEROT for work under 1st Home Counties Field Company, R.E. respectively. The 2 platoons left at HAVRE, joined the Bn. at 9 pm.

Appendix.

Geographical series Gen. Staff No. 2743.

20th.

The Commanding Officer spent the day in C lines section 4 having spent the night at C lines Head Quarters. The following casualties occurred in the trenches in No.15 Platoon from rifle fire Killed at 6.45 a.m. No. 1664 Pte. Phillips, J.E. slightly wounded at 8.30 a.m. No.2295 Pte. Carter A.J. Private Phillips was buried in the trenches.
About 3 p.m. Head Quarters "C" lines was shelled and burnt to the ground. In the fire the rifles and kits of half the men of the 2 platoons in reserve were destroyed. All the possessions of Capt. Cossar & 2.Lt. Chennell were also destroyed.
A German aeroplane passed over H.Q. going W. about 8.30 a.m. & returned about 9 a.m. A few shells

1915.

March.   Appendix.

20th.
(Ctd).
fell in the neighbourhood of
H.Q. about 4 p.m.
Working parties of 100 men
under Capt. Smith & 150 men
under Capt. Tully reported
xxxxxxxxxxx the former at 7 pm.
and the latter at 6.30 pm. the
respective rendezvous being
Road Junc. Sq. M.22.b.8.8. &
M.22 central to work under 15th
Field Coy. R.E. & 1st Home
Counties R.E.

21st.
At 2 pm. the Battalion marched
back to LA GORGUE and took over
fresh billets. The 4 platoons
from the trenches and the 2
reserve platoons attached to
the 2nd Middx. did not arrive
until after midnight. The
former had sustained one casualty
in Lt. Hurd's platoon No.
Pte. Sweetsur. The 2 platoons
in reserve had been heavily
shelled in the afternoon but had
sustained no casualties.

LA GORGUE.

22nd.
Kept as a rest day. Orders were
received to move to SAILLY
tomorrow in order to take over
trenches held by Canadian
Division on the 25th.

23rd.
About midday a waggon load of
hand grenades blew up in "C" Coys.
billeting areas seriously injuring
Cpl. Knewers P. and an N.C.O.
attached from the 2nd Battn. at
2 p.m. the Battn. moved off to
take over fresh billets at
BAC ST. MAUR.

BAC ST. MAUR.

24th.
At 9.30 a.m. a conference was
held at Bde.H.Q. to explain
arrangements for taking over
section 4 of the trench line
now held by the 8th Canadian
Regt.   During the afternoon
the Battn. staff and representative
Officers visited the trenches
personally to acquaint themselves
with the arrangements there.

1915.

March.   Appendix.

25th.   At 5.30 p.m. the Battn.
                    marched via FLEURBAIX and
                    CROIX MARECHAL to take over
                    section 4 of the trench line
                    at LA BOUTILLERIE. At 8.30 pm.
                    the relief of the 8th Canadian
                    Rgt. had been effected. "C"
                    Coy. held portion of trenches
                    on our right of main road, "D"
                    Coy. with Machine Gun section
                    the remainder. "A" Coy. was
                    in support "B" Coy. in reserve
                    both billeted along the road.
                    Head Quarters at large farm at
                    LA BOUTILLERIE. The transport
                    which moved at 4 pm. was parked
                    along the Rue de 1 PIERRE. The
                    Grenadier Platoon (1 N.C.O. &
                    5 men per Company) was formed
                    this day under 2.Lt. Chennell
                    and marched & remained with
                    the Transport. Lieut. H.K.King
                    went into Hospital this day.

                    LA BOUTILLERIE.

26th.   The Major commanding supporting
                    Battery called at 10.30 a.m.
                    At 11 a.m. the Brigade Major
                    and Adjutant 6th Scottish
                    Rifles called to discuss
                    arrangements for instruction of
                    that Battn. in trench duties.
                    At 3.30 pm Major
                    Commanding 15th Field Company R.E.
                    visited the trenches. At 4 pm
                    representatives of 6th Scottish
                    Rifles visited the trenches.
                    The same Battn. handed over 4
                    periscopes. In the trenches
                    no unusual occurrence took
                    place during the 24 hours. During
                    the day one man No. 1422 Pte. Watt,
                    G. was severely wounded.

27th.   Nothing to report from trenches
                    No. 3675 Pte. Thompson W.F.
                    D.Coy. accidentally wounded.
                    At 10 am. O.O. took O.C. and
                    Adjt. 6th Scottish Rifles round
                    the trenches and defended
                    localities. Col. Hayes and
                    Brigade Major also visited trenches.
                    During afternoon between 4 & 5 pm
                    the area was shelled by enemy's
                    howitzers for one hour. About
                    30 shells fell at first in
                    neighbourhood of H.Q. afterwards
                    in front of nearest billets.
                    No damage was done. During the
                    evening 4 platoons 6th Scottish
                    Rifles entered the trenches for the

1915.

March.   Appendix.

27th.   night. Pte. Watts died of
(Ctd).   his wounds this day.

28th.   Nothing to report from trenches.
             One casualty No. 3817 Pte.
             Markwick who was killed. During
             the evening "A" Coy. relieved "C"
             Coy. in right section & "B"
             relieved "D" in left section. Four
             platoons from 6th Scottish Rifles
             again visited the trenches.
             Report received that Cpl. Knowers
             died on his way to Hospital on
             22nd & was buried at MERVILLE.

29th.   Nothing to Report. No casualties.
             Four platoons 6th Scottish Rifles
             spent night in trenches.

30th.   Nothing to Report. One man
             slightly wounded. Lce.Cpl.
             Pendleton "B" Coy. Pte.Kittle,
             "D" Coy. accidentally shot himself
             in foot. Four platoons 6th Scottish
             Rifles went into trenches for the
             night. Orders received to take
             over Billets of 6th Scottish
             Rifles tomorrow who will replace
             us in the trenches.

31st.   At 8 a.m. the General inspected
             the trenches. 2.Lt. Ronald M.E.
             King was nominated as an assistant
             A.D.C. In the evening the Battalion
             was relieved by the 6th Scottish
             Rifles and moved into the Billets
             of that Battn.H.Q. and A & D.Coys.
             in FLEURBAIX. B & C Coys. on
             RUE DEL PIERRE.

                                    G.A.H. BOWER, Capt. & Adj.
                                    1/7 Middlesex Regt.

WAR DIARY
or
INTELLIGENCE SUMMARY.
(Erase heading not required.)

Army Form C. 2118.

Place	Date	Hour	Summary of Events and Information	Remarks and references to Appendices
Avonmouth	4.iii.15	4 am	Landed at Avonmouth from Gibraltar and proceeded to High Barnet.	
High Barnet	7.iii.15	6 pm	Reported mobilization completed and ready to move.	
do	10.iii.15	12 noon	Received orders, "Hold yourself in readiness to move dicey."	
do	do	10 pm	Received Southampton (6 say) 12th	
do	12.iii.15		Proceeded Knebworth Station [for Southampton] Trains left Knebworth at 7.30 am, 9.10 am + 10.50 am. Entrained on S.S. Newhaven and left Southampton 9.30 pm proceeding without escort. Strength 26 officers and 811 other ranks. Transport into 4 officers and 96 other ranks on the "Inventor". Later ship travelled under escort.	
Havre	13.iii.15	6.15 am	Disembarked and marched to No 2. Rest Camp at Bleville (BLEVILLE). Transport and detachment from "Inventor" joining later in the day. Completed deficiencies in equipment. The Interpreter Decormis (No. 45 "Inventoire" Infantry regiment) reported for duty. Received orders to entrain tomorrow [17?] 2 platoons first.	

1577 Wt. W10791/1773 500,000 1/15 D. D. & L. A.D.S.S./Forms/C. 2118.

WAR DIARY
INTELLIGENCE SUMMARY
(Erase heading not required.)

Army Form C. 2118.

Place	Date	Hour	Summary of Events and Information	Remarks and references to Appendices
LE HAVRE	14.11.15	1 pm	Battalion entrained at Havre leaving station at 4.30 pm. Two platoons (Nos 3 + 4) left at rest camp [Lieuts Roy & 85 NCOs & men] under 2/Lt. Nesbit and 2/Lt R. Chalklen also Lt-Philpin Orderly Room Sergeant [N.H.K. Knapp] 4 sick men and 3 drummers under age [their strength therefore 28 officers & men]	
LA GORGUE	15.11.15	1.30 pm	Arrived at LA GORGUE [and moved into billets. A Coy (less 2 platoons), "C" Coy + H.Q. at Ferme l'Abbé detrn at school D Coy and transport at Rue de Gendarmerie, H.Q. in House next to Post Office.] Attached 23rd Brigade VIII Division 4 Corps	
do	16.11.15		Returned battalion cooks to ordnance.	
do	17.11.15	8 am	Received orders known at 11 am and go into fresh billets in neighbourhood of LA FLINQUE. H.Q. and C + D Companies on road E of LA FLINQUE. A + B on Road S.W. of LA FLINQUE. The Battalion was met by the Brigade Commander General PINNEY	

WAR DIARY
or
INTELLIGENCE SUMMARY
(Erase heading not required.)

Army Form C. 2118.

Hour, Date, Place	Summary of Events and Information	Remarks and references to Appendices
17.iii.15.	After leaving LE DRUMEZ and deploying to Divisional Commander General DAVIES. The Transport was parked on road 1½ miles W of LA FLINQUE. General Plumer visited the troops in their billets in the afternoon. Exchanged 2 NCOs & privates per platoon with 2/1st Battn & attached further Lafant Plays for instructional purposes. Meanwhile Platoon Commanders when having their men engaged throwing dummy bombs in improving country. Brigade and subsidiary reserves. During the afternoon the transport lines were subjected to shell fire. 38 shells having in the line between languages from or near DRUMEZ. Transport was moved back to LE DRUMEZ at 6.30 pm 2 platoons under 2nd Lt H.P. Williamson reported at cross roads S.E. of B in BACQUEROT to work under 15th Field Company R.E. "B" Coy reported at crossroads South	
LA FLINGUE 18.iii.15		Map Sheet 36. 1:40,000. LILLE. Ruined Systems of Germany

(3.)

WAR DIARY

INTELLIGENCE SUMMARY.
(Erase heading not required.)

Army Form C. 2118.

Hour, Date, Place	Summary of Events and Information	Remarks and references to Appendices
(4)		
LA FLINQUE 18/3/15	R in RUE du ACQUEROT from R under 1st Hants bounties billed by R.E.	map sheet 36 1/40,000 French system of survey geographical series Sheet No 27.J.3
LA FLINQUE 19/3/15	C.O. and adjutant attended a conference at H.Q. "C" Coy. and at 9 am each coy/coy. was ordered to detach completion to accompany companies of the 2nd Wiltshires to relieve duty in the trenches. Except at 2 midnight 4/2 at 6.30 pm. Platoons detailed. Officers A Coy, 2nd Lieutenants A.G. & D. T. Smith, C Coy & Lt Shorto. B. Coy. Captain Court with 4th Kings Liverpool platoons was ordered to take up two as reinforcement attached and tune of "C" Lines. Each man was to be armed with 2 empty sandbags # 2 equipped with ammunition, 100 rounds extra ammunition Gas-protector hardwick. nashfer Capt. Hort & B. Coy. Capt. Moody "A" Coy + Flight Scott.	

WAR DIARY
INTELLIGENCE SUMMARY.
(Erase heading not required.)

Army Form C. 2118.

Hour, Date, Place	Summary of Events and Information	Remarks and references to Appendices
LA FLINQUE 20.iii.16	First R.Cp. were attached corresponding to 2 pickelax left 48 hours duty Katanches for individuals, supplies reporting at 4 fm. Two working parties of 100 men under Lieuts Ash & Somers under Capt Jolly were transported at 6.30 pm at Rouds Junction M22 & 28 for work under 15 Field Coy R.E. and at M22 central RUE du BACQUEROT for work under 1st Harv. Coy Field Company R.E. respectively. The Commanding officer spent the day in C line's section & having spent the night in C lines their Quarters Hythstery Quadrilateral occurred in it stands No 15t Mortary from rifle fire killed at 6.45 am No. 1664 Pte Phillips.J.E.Signed HPhillips Pte Cartee,G.T. Private Newsome was buried in Hazebrouck	The platoon left at Harve respectively. Both stay in sec. at 6.10 am No. 2295 Signed.

WAR DIARY
INTELLIGENCE SUMMARY
(Erase heading not required.)

Army Form C. 2118.

Instructions regarding War Diaries and Intelligence Summaries are contained in F.S. Regs., Part II and the Staff Manual respectively. Title pages will be prepared in manuscript.

Hour, Date, Place	Summary of Events and Information	Remarks and references to Appendices
LA FLINQUE 20.iii.15	About 3 p.m. Germans shelled our front trenches & the first 3 rifles and kits of half the men of the 2 platoons in reserve which stayed, all the possessions of officers & men were destroyed. Germans aeroplane passed over H.Q. going W. about 8.30 a.m. Trenches which G & H. Co. Trenches hit in several places. H.Q. about 4 p.m. Working parties of 100 men under Capt & 150 men under Capt Tully report to Sapoline the Sorerment of Nieuwe Keeny Post Tom. Sq M22 B88 & M22 central rendezvous. 15 1st Field Coy R.E. At 8 p.m. Horne took over P.E.	[illegible remarks]
LA FLINQUE 21.3.15	At 2 p.m. the Battalion under Lt. Col. L.A. GORGIE and took over front billets from the trenches and the 2 reserve platoons.	

Army Form C. 2118.

WAR DIARY
— or —
INTELLIGENCE SUMMARY.
(Erase heading not required.)

Instructions regarding War Diaries and Intelligence Summaries are contained in F.S. Regs., Part II and the Staff Manual respectively. Title pages will be prepared in manuscript.

(1)

Hour, Date, Place	Summary of Events and Information	Remarks and references to Appendices
LA GORGUE ATTING 22.iii.15	attached. After 2nd billets did not arrive until after midnight. The former had contained cavalry in fact its latrine no: Protestant. The platoons in consequence had been heavily shelled in the afternoon but had sustained no casualties.	
LA GORGUE 23.iii.15	Kept on areas day. Letters have required change of BILLEY [reserved in order that the Brigades [ill.] be forwarded. Division on the 25th. About midday a wagon load of hand grenades blew up in "C" Coys billeting area seriously injuring [Pte Knowles?] and one NCO attached from the 2nd Bath.] At 2pm the Bath moved off to take over [illegible] at BAC St MAUR.	
BAC ST MAUR 24.iii.15	At 9.30am a conference was held at Bde HQ to explain arrangements for taking over sections of the trenches then northern by the Canadian Regt. During the afternoon billets & oh also were inspected. Their suitability towards personnel of inspected billets with the arrangements for...	

WAR DIARY
INTELLIGENCE SUMMARY.
(Erase heading not required.)

Army Form C. 2118.

Hour, Date, Place	Summary of Events and Information	Remarks and references to Appendices
BAC ST MAUR 25.iii.15	At 5.30 p.m. the Batt: marched via FLEUR BAIX and CROIX MARECHAL to take over section of the trenches line at LA BOUTILLERIE. At 9.30 p.m. the relief of the 8 Canadian Rifles was effected. "C" Coy took the portion of trenches on our right of main road, "D" Coy with machine gun section the remainder. "B" Coy in reserve but billeted along terraced Headquarters at large farm at LA BOUTILLERIE. The transport which moved at 4 p.m. was halted along the Rue de PIERRE. The Grenadier Platoon (1 NCO & 5 men per company) was formed this day (under 2/Lt. Chitwell) and marched independent with the transport. Lieut H.F. Kent went with hospital staff. The Major commanding supporting Battery called at 10.30 a.m. Capt Hare, the Brigadier Major and Adjutant C.F. Potters Rifle Batten Scot	
LA BOUTILLERIE 26.iii.15		

WAR DIARY / INTELLIGENCE SUMMARY

Army Form C. 2118.

Hour, Date, Place	Summary of Events and Information	Remarks and references to Appendices
LA BOUTILLERIE 26. iii. 15	Means arrangements for instructions of but Batt'n in trench duties. at 3.30 p.m. Major commanding 15th Field Company R.E. visited the trenches. At 4 p.m. representatives of the 6th Scottish Rifles visited the trenches. The same hour handed over 4 Minenwerfen & Attenuation. No unusual occurrences took place during the 24 hours. During today one man No. 11422 Pte. Watt, G. was accidentally wounded.	
do 27. iii. 15	Nothing to report from trenches. Rifle Shortage. M.G. O.C. and Adjt. 6th Scottish Rifles round the trenches and defended localities. Capt. Hayes and Brigade Major also visited trenches. During afternoon between 4 to 7 p.m. the area was shelled by enemy's howitzers. One shell fell about in neighbourhood of H.Q. afterwards in front of garrot killets. No damage.	

WAR DIARY
INTELLIGENCE SUMMARY.
(Erase heading not required.)

Army Form C. 2118.

Hour, Date, Place	Summary of Events and Information	Remarks and references to Appendices
LA BOUILLERIE 28.iii.15	Two down. During the evening 4 platoons 6th Scottish rifles entered the trenches for the night. Reports died of his wounds this day.	
29.iii.15	Nothing to report from trenches. Pte [Greenhalgh] No 3817 Pte [Marchbank who was] killed. During the evening "A" Coy relieved "C" Coy in right section of advance. "B" in left section. Four platoons of 6th Scottish Rifles relieved four platoons of 6th Scottish Rifles. Report received that the Germans shelled a Report received at 2.30 two miles at MERVILLE. No Coy killed. McCausland. Four platoons 6th Scottish Rifles spent night in trenches	
30.iii.15	Nothing to report. One man slightly wounded. Two Coys of Scottish accidentally by Rifle. B Coy & C Coy in front line. Two Platoons 6th Scottish Rifles were sent back into trenches to-night & took over billets of 4 platoons of this Corps when relieved on the trenches	

Army Form C. 2118.

WAR DIARY
INTELLIGENCE SUMMARY.
(Erase heading not required.)

Instructions regarding War Diaries and Intelligence Summaries are contained in F.S. Regs., Part II and the Staff Manual respectively. Title pages will be prepared in manuscript.

Hour, Date, Place	Summary of Events and Information	Remarks and references to Appendices
31.iii.15	At 4 a.m. the General inspected the trenches. 2/Lt Ronald H.E. King was commissioned and was appointed A.D.C. In the evening the Battalion was relieved by the 9th Middlesex Regt. and moved into the billets of that Regt. Hd. and "D" Coys in FLEURBAIX. "B" Coys in RUE DEL PIERRE.	[signatures] Lieut. Col. Commdg. 1st BATT. 7th MIDDLESEX REGT.

8TH DIVISION
23RD INFY BDE

1-7TH BN MIDDX REGT
FEB 1915-JAN 1916   TO { 56 DIV
                             167 Bde

~~1-8TH BN MIDDX REGT~~
{ AUG 1915
{ SEP "

FROM UK
───────────────
TO 56 DIV — 167 BDE

{ 8 DIV   25 BDE   1915 MAR - JUN
{ 23 DIV   70 BDE   1915 AUG - 1916 JAN
{ 8   167   1916 FEB - 1919 ...

Copies to:-
1. Commanding Officer.
2. O.C. "A" Co.
3. " "B" Co.
4. " "C" "
5. " "D" "
6. O.C.2/Devon Regt.
7. Q.M.& T.O.
8. O.C. H.Qtrs Co.
9. O.C.2/W.Yorks Regt.
10. H Qtrs 23rd Inf.Bde.
11. Adjutant.
12. I.O.
13. 2/Lieut.Glover.
14. Office.